HELPING
HOWARD

HELPING HOWARD

A NOVEL

SALLY SCHLOSS

atmosphere press

For David

"Writing means revealing oneself to excess."
Franz Kafka, *Letters to Felice*, 1913

"We are well advised to keep on nodding terms with the people we used to be, whether we find them attractive company or not."
Joan Didion, *Slouching Towards Bethlehem*

AUTHOR'S NOTE

This is a novel in which the main character, Howard, helps The Author write a book, and The Author in turn helps Howard understand his marriage.

HELPING HOWARD
MAY 1999

How can I help you today, Howard?

Howard groaned and kicked back the covers and hated the fact that he was now cold when a moment before he was nice and warm in bed.

You can help me by letting me go back to sleep.

Can't do that, Howard. Lots to do today.

Yeah? Like what?

I need you to start my novel.

What's in it for me?

You get a reason to get out of bed.

Will I fall in love today?

Maybe. Don't know yet.

Will I eat something I like?

Yes, I can give you that.

Okay. What do I like?

You tell me.

Let me think about it. Okay. I want pancakes with butter and maple syrup.

Fine. That's what you'll have then.

What's the weather like?

What kind of weather do you like?

I want sunny and not hot. I'd say around sixty degrees. Bright blue sky.

Well, surprise! That's what it's like outside today.

You're just saying that to get me out of bed.

No, I'm not. It's really a beautiful day. Get up and see for yourself.

Howard groaned again. *Now what?*

Now you get up and pee and take a shower and get dressed and go downstairs for your pancakes.

Do we need all these details?

No. Not really.

Is anything going to happen today?

I don't know yet. What do you want to have happen?

What anyone would want to have happen; I would like to fall in love, have great sex, have a brilliant life and live happily ever after.

Not going to happen, Howard.

Why not?

Boring. Boring to read about. Besides, it's a total fantasy and I don't write fantasy fiction.

You're not going to hurt me, are you?

You mean physically?

We can start with that.

I wasn't planning on it. There may be a car accident or maybe a plane crash.

Okay, then I'm going back to bed.

No. Okay. No physical pain.

Good. Last time you put me in a building that collapsed, and I nearly died. You described every gruesome detail about how I looked and how shitty I felt.

Howard, I made you famous. Quit complaining.

Howard Blackman got out of bed and briefly glanced at his wife of fifteen years, a woman with whom he'd had sex approximately ten times in the last thirteen.

Nice. You're starting already.

He pushed his feet into his boiled wool slippers that he loved, a gift from his daughter last Chanukah, and stood up feeling stiff and old.

You said no pain.

Just a little pain. It'll go away as soon as you move around a bit.

Can I at least be good-looking?

Howard ran his fingers through his thick, wavy, salt-and-pepper hair, the envy of all his male friends and a female head-turner. All the women thought, "sexy," as soon as they saw it.

Happy?

Not bad.

Howard walked into the bathroom and looked in the mirror, feeling much better about the morning as soon as he evaluated his reflection. He smiled at himself because he always looked better, younger, when he smiled. He saw his intense, dark blue eyes, with their self-mocking regard, and the pleas-

5

ing creases around his mouth. He had bright white teeth, courtesy of Dr. Shulman, his dentist. He turned in profile, lifted his pajama top, and inspected his flat stomach and surprisingly muscular chest. He had thickened over the years, but not fattened.

Okay. That's enough. You don't have to go overboard on this. How good can I look, I'm what? Forty-five? Fifty?

Let's make you fifty-three. You married late.

Why did I do that?

You were afraid of commitment.

I was? You're making this up.

Yes.

Can't you make up something else?

Like what?

That I hadn't found the right woman yet? That I waited for years and then I met her?

Okay. Where were you when you met?

Living in Manhattan.

What were you doing?

I was working in a small design firm, playing out on weekends.

You were a musician?

Yes.

What instrument?

Drums.

Were you any good?

Not good enough apparently. Look where I am now.

Where are you?

Living in the "burbs" of New Jersey with a woman who supports me and doesn't have sex with me, and a daughter that I raised myself practically, and who now barely talks to me.

Why is that?

How the hell should I know? She's fifteen.

Boyfriend?

Not that I know of.

But you wouldn't know, would you, Howard? You just said she doesn't talk to you.

Thanks. Rub it in.

Howard, we have to get on with the story.

Why is my name Howard? Howard is such a dorky name.

I'm not good at names.

Why can't I be Cameron, or Blade?

It's too late, you're Howard.

Why? Why is it too late?

Because, we've already begun the story, and you're already Howard. I already have a lot invested in Howard. Besides, it would confuse our readers if you suddenly became Maxwell.

We have readers?

Howard went downstairs and saw that it was a gorgeous fall day. He whipped batter in a bowl, heated the syrup, and nuked the butter.

I don't like microwaves. I would never have one.

He heated the syrup and melted the butter in a pan on the top of their fancy-assed, energy efficient, environmentally and politically correct stove.

Is the pan aluminum or stainless steel?

Thinking about the song he was working on in his head, he reached out to grab the small, cast iron pan, but didn't think to grab a mitt and realized his mistake when he closed his fingers around the scorching handle.

You're a vindictive, sick person, you know that?

Howard's scream could be heard by his wife all the way upstairs in their nice quiet bedroom overlooking the brook that ran behind their house and through their acre of land. She mumbled, "Howard, are you all right?" and then fell back to sleep.

His daughter, unbeknownst to either parent, wasn't home, so she wasn't there to hear her father's screams. She hadn't been home all night.

I'd like to go back to meeting my wife in New York. When she still wanted sex with me.

I hate to tell you Howard, but she never really wanted sex with you.

What are you talking about? We had sex all the time. We had sex with other women. We had orgies.

She was in her bisexual phase. She didn't know what she was doing.

I know, I know. She's gay.

I think the more interesting story, Howard, is why you've stayed with her all these years.

Yeah, that's not the story I want to tell.

Okay. We'll compromise. It will be both stories. How you met and fell in love and then what happened and why you stayed.

But I don't know why I stayed.

You don't have to know, Howard. Only the reader has to know.

You keep saying that. I think that's your fantasy, that we have readers.

Howard Blackman was thirty-six-years-old when he met Cynthia.

Nope. Don't like Cynthia.

Okay, Howard, what do you want your wife's name to be?

T. J.

That's a name?

Yeah.

What's it stand for?

Don't know. I forget. Ask her.

Howard Blackman was thirty-six-years-old when he met T.J. at the Halloween party his design firm threw in their loft space. She showed up with his friend Greg. She came as a whore and Greg was her pimp. When the song "Walking the Dog" came on, T.J. and Greg parted the crowd with their performance. T.J. humped Greg's leg as he strutted down an imaginary sidewalk, looking left, looking right, then patted the top of her head. She squatted in her black leather mini skirt and fishnet stockings, balancing on her three-inch stiletto heels and bent her head under his hand as he stroked her shaggy red and black hair.

"Walkin' the dog. Justa walkin' the dog. If you don't know how to do it, I'll show you how to walk the dog."

Howard was impressed by her moves. She was very...agile.

Howard was a Hari Krishna. He wore a flesh-colored, latex skullcap that completely covered his hair and made his ears stick out. He wore a saffron-dyed bed sheet, belted with a rope. Even though he was freezing his nuts off, he wore Jesus sandals and only his BVDs underneath.

"Hari Krishna, Hari Krishna, Krishna, Krishna, Hari Hari," he sang, dancing and twirling around, grinning idiotically while clanging his finger cymbals together.

I'll let "grinning idiotically" pass. I know you meant to imply that I was in character.

Exactly.

"So," Howard said, clapping his finger cymbals in her face, "you're a working girl?"

She gave him a long, appraising look. "I'm not into freaks," she said.

"You mean you are not a spiritual person?" he said in a thick Indian accent. "I am thinking I would like to invite you to one of our parties where you can meet other nice young people."

"I don't do parties. I'm strictly one-on-one, or a three-way if it's with another woman." She blew pot smoke in his face. While they were talking, her pimp, Greg, had passed her a joint.

I like the part about the three ways. You're finally doing something nice for me.

"What do you do when you're not being a prostitute?"

"I photograph prostitutes."

"Really? I think that's great."

"Why?" T.J. moved her face closer to his, practically sneering.

"I like that you photograph women at risk, women who are vulnerable and held in contempt. I think it's admirable. Makes these women relatable, shows their humanity."

"Not exactly, asshole. I photograph them cause I think they're pretty." She moved off in another cloud of smoke, repeating the word "relatable" and chuckling.

You hate me.

I don't hate you. I actually have sympathy for you.

Where? Where's the sympathy?

We'll get to that.

It was drizzling out and Howard was standing on the corner of Houston and Sullivan when he saw a woman with short, black and red hair crossing the street gingerly, running on her tip toes to avoid puddles. She was wearing cargo pants and a t-shirt, and because her shirt was damp and she wore no bra, he could see her nipples and the outline of her bouncing breasts. After the last car whizzed by, she sprinted and wound up a few feet from him. She was holding a Leica in her hand.

"T.J.?"

She turned and noticed him, raised the camera to her face and took a picture.

"Why would you photograph me? I'm not a prostitute."

"You're not?" T.J. smiled. "Then what are you?"

He liked her wispy, choppy hair, and lean boy's body. Without makeup, her face was angular and pale. She was slender, but strong; like a gazelle.

"I was a Hare Krishna. From the Halloween party. Your rejection ignited my spiritual crisis and I left the cult. I've stopped begging at airports."

She laughed. "Yes. Yes. I remember." She held out her camera-free hand. "Nice to see you again."

Howard shook it, saying, "So, you really are a photographer. Was the rest true?"

"I'm sure it was." She fiddled with the camera. "What did I say?"

"Why don't I tell you over a cup of coffee? The Cupping

Room's not far."

The drizzling had made the short tendrils of her hair curl and press against her cheeks and forehead. He pictured her in bed, sweaty after sex, her hair looking just like that. He wanted to be in bed with her right that second.

"Wish I could. I have a thing in about twenty minutes."

"No you don't."

"What?"

"It's an excuse. 'A thing.'"

She looked at him, studying. He was easily fifteen, twenty years older than her.

He was wearing khakis and a blue striped shirt open at the collar. He had a canvas book bag over his shoulder. He was wearing a Yankees baseball cap. Sneakers.

Not how his father dressed approaching forty. Thank God for the sixties. He knew he was a handsome man. He didn't have the handsome man, "droit de signeur," look but he did have the confidence to be pushy. Women liked him. For awhile.

For awhile? Why for awhile? What's wrong with me?

That's for me to know, and you to find out.

You don't know, do you?

Well, I have some idea.

Some idea? You're going to put me through something torturous while you figure it out?

It's how I learn things. How I learn what I know.

That's great for you. But I'm having the experience, and I'm in the dark here.

Like real life.

T.J. shrugged and didn't smooth over or explain. This actually excited him. He liked women that were hard to secure, that kept him off balance and wanting them. He knew he was fucked up, but the rush was what mattered. He needed it to get interested and stay interested. Long term though, it pretty much destroyed him.

"Okay, well, how about this. I'm playing at Café Wha? and would love you to come. Friday night at 9:00 p.m."

"What kind of music?"

"Bluesy rock."

She still hesitated.

"I'll pay you to take pictures."

"How much?"

"Friend rate?"

"We're not friends."

"Friends of friends rate then?"

She smiled again. She had a cocky smile. She was a tough cookie. But she was young. He knew he had the advantage. Check. Mate.

You make me sound predatory. Calculating.

Oh, come on. This is a game. Of course you're measuring, seeking advantage. You've had more experience. Gives older men an edge.

Really? I thought young women had all the power. We're just worms seeking a way in.

You said it, not me, buster.

Will the worm turn in this story?

Maybe. Don't know yet.

Yes, you do.

She furrowed her brow. "Okay." She fished a business card out of her pants pocket.

He smiled, looking at it. It was dog-eared and bent. But it had her phone number on it.

"Call me," she said, "gotta go," and strode off.

He stood there watching her walk away, evaluating. She was long-legged and moved from the hips and shoulders. Not a lot of ass swaying. He looked at the black and white photo on the card—smoke from a cigarette against a black background— T.J. Photographer and her number. No last name. He raised the card to his nose and sniffed, but there was nothing, no scent of her. He stuck the card in his shirt pocket and walked off whistling.

God! You make me sound like a pervert.

What are you talking about? Look, you're whistling. You're a happy man.

This isn't going to go well. You're setting me up.

Howard, stop complaining. You're gonna get laid, aren't you? It's what you want, isn't it?

Yes.

Howard called her and they arranged a price for the photo shoot of his band, Mud, a name meant to evoke their earthy, dank sound with its swampy, decaying groove. This was the voice of moonless nights and solitary confinement, of bullfrogs desperately calling for mates.

Jesus Christ.

What?

I'm a white, Jewish guy from Brooklyn.

But you want to be cool, Howard. And there's a part of you that's dark and very lonely.

I don't feel that part.

That's the problem. But, it does come out in your music.

14

Besides, everybody else in the band is black. You bring the iro-ny. They bring the soul.

Are we any good?

Some nights better than others. But not bad. Not fame worthy. But talented enough. I actually like how bleak the songs are.

You would. How were we the night T.J. showed up?

I'd say that was your best gig. You delivered. All that adrenaline and desire to make her want you elevated your per-formance. You were slick on that stage and the vibe was conta-gious.

Camera bulb flashes went off in Howard's face and he turned toward the light to get a glimpse of T.J. She was crouched near the stage, shooting from below, and then she was on his left, snapping away. He made eye contact and grinned at her as his drumsticks hit hard on the downbeat.

"Stick around," he called to T.J. from the stage just after the set ended. She nodded, sitting alone at a table. As they broke down and packed up, he glanced over to make sure she hadn't bolted. After a few words to his band mates he finally headed her way.

"You were good."

"As in me?" he said, pointing at his chest and taking a seat.

"Yes. And the band. I like how depressed the music sound-ed. Your songs?"

"I wrote *Country Song.*"

"Which one was that?"

He started singing, not quite on key, a bit rough. He didn't have a great voice, but it was fine for background vocals.

"He's in a country band
And still livin' on the land
Hates the state he's livin' in
Getting old and wearing thin
Had some women in his prime
Loretta, Sue, and Clementine
All good lookin', all sweet things
'Til he beat them and turned mean
No, he's not a violent guy
Mostly moonshine makes him cry
But when women want too much
Makes him angry, makes him tough
And the moment when she leaves
He acts hard, but then he grieves
Drinking, swearing through the night
Wishing he had made it right
No one special, no one close
It's himself he hates the most
Still goes out to pick and sing
But his life is not his dream
What's the answer? Who's to blame?
Living life as living pain
There've been good times in the past
Never learned to make them last
What's the reason to go on?
Life's a moment marathon.
Life's a moment marathon."

He stopped the waitress as she was passing with a tray of drinks. "Guinness, please," he said, then looked back at T.J.

She nodded. "Make that two."

She took a pack of cigarettes from her jacket pocket and a book of matches, tapped out one and lit it. He hated smoking. He hated the smell. He couldn't imagine kissing her now.

"So, why are you so depressed?"

"I'm not."

"Oh."

"Look," he said, "it's a shitty world for lots of people. I have a good imagination. It's not me."

"Sure." She twisted the side of her mouth into a half-smirk. She looked cute.

"I've never even been to the country."

She laughed.

"What about you?" he asked.

"Me? I guess. Sometimes. More like a melancholy, but it doesn't last."

"Melancholy about what?"

"Well, not just melancholy, a kind of nostalgia."

"For what?"

She paused, fiddling with her cigarette, considering. She had movie star fingers, elegantly long and thin. No nail polish, though, and now that he was looking, he noticed the skin on some had been chewed. She was a biter.

The drinks arrived and both of them waved away the offer of glasses.

"At the risk of sounding like an idiot," she said, "I feel nostalgia for a world I've never known. Like all my life I've lived behind a curtain with an eye-hole and I'm observing."

He leaned toward her. "What happens when you look away?"

"I realize the world has nothing to do with me. But I'm fascinated by it. And when I close my eyes I miss it."

"'No direction home,'" Howard said.

She looked at him, impressed. "Yes. 'Like a complete unknown.'"

"'Like a rolling stone.'"

Howard raised his bottle of Guinness and she raised hers. "Dylan," he said, and they clinked bottles.

At that moment they heard gunshots. She whipped her head around to see what was happening. Howard jumped up, pulled her to her feet, and threw a protective arm around her. They heard people running in the streets and the club was now in chaos.

"Don't people usually duck?" she asked into his shoulder, flinging her cigarette to the floor and securing her camera around her neck, but she didn't resist as he led her to the back of the club and the Ladies Room, closing the door behind them and flipping the switch. It was small, too tight for two people. Still he didn't have his arm around her now.

"Is this safe?"

"Yes," he said, having no idea if it was true.

Her face looked like a clenched fist. He was flooded with adrenaline and wondered how he looked.

"I could be shooting this."

"Yeah, and maybe get shot. You want that? You want to go back out there?"

"You don't need to protect me."

"Sounds like I do. If not from some maniac, then from yourself and your bad impulses."

"Like you would know my impulses."

"I know you're self-destructive."

"What?"

"You smoke."

"That's a ridiculous thing to say."

"I don't like smoking."

"Who cares what you like?"

"Well, it's deadly. Just takes longer."

"Yes, dad."

That stung.

"I suppose you don't have any bad habits. You're Mister Clean."

"Of course I have bad habits."

"Name one."

"I take willful children into small Ladies Rooms and lecture them for their own good."

That made her smile. "Not just me then?"

"No, I do this all the time."

She laughed. "I guess you staged the shooting." She stopped and listened, hearing the approach of sirens. "I wonder what the fuck happened."

It was quiet in the club now on the other side of the door. Maybe everyone had fled, or were out on the sidewalk being questioned by the police. Maybe someone was dead or injured.

His bravado was all to impress, but also something more primal had been stirred—a need to protect the girl.

"Why aren't you scared?" he asked.

"I don't know. I suppose I should be. It feels more like heightened awareness, with a kick of anxiety that makes me want to run out and witness."

"Instead of hiding?"

"Right."

"Then why are you here?"

"You stopped me, remember?"

"You could have ignored me."

"I was caught up in the moment."

She tapped another cigarette out of the pack and put it to her lips.

"Don't."

"Why not?"

"Let me offer you a different solution." He took her chin in his hand and kissed her. Very much to his surprise, she kissed him back.

I like this. Don't stop here. I want to know what happens.

You already know what happens. You get married to T.J.

Yeah, but I want all the courtship scenes, all the sex and desire. All the good stuff.

Howard, I choose what's important to include.

But I want to choose too.

You can't. Authors have to have control of their characters.

Well, that sucks.

I'll tell you what happened.

Show, don't tell. No one's gonna read this.

You had a nice civil ceremony at City Hall. Both your best friends were there.

What about parents?

Yours are dead and T.J. is estranged from hers.

How convenient.

Yes. Not relevant to the story.

Families are always relevant to the story. To quote Philip Larkin,

"They fuck you up, your mum and dad.
They may not mean to, but they do.
They fill you with the faults they had
And add some extra, just for you."
Yes, so we'll learn about the parents through their children.
I want children.
You do?
Will I have any?
Not if you don't let me get on with the story.
You said you would help me.
I'm listening.

Just give me something. Just one tiny scene about me from her point-of-view. Why did she go home with me, and one, just one experience that proves we were happy.

Why?

Because, I want to remember our being happy.

T.J.

After the gunshots, when Howard jumped up and threw a protective arm around her, an old feeling surfaced. She supposed it was his age that made her think of her father; maybe it was his tucking her under his arm like a child.

When he kissed her, however, that didn't come as a surprise. She'd known he was attracted to her; he'd been coming onto her since they'd met. What did surprise her was her reaction to his kiss. Other than her father, an older man had never kissed her on the mouth. Of course, she'd been with a few men, but they were all her age.

Her response was ardent and unexpected. Not that she hadn't been aroused by his attraction; man or woman, being desired was a turn on, a form of narcissism she supposed, like being seduced by your own reflection. But if the attraction didn't start with her, boredom would quickly set in. No, it was only the ones she chose, the ones she desired, that brought on the sustained fever, drug-swift and out-of-control. By twenty-two she'd had her heart broken only once. Cleo, an older woman, was cruel and the sex turned sadistic. Still, it took her a year to leave, and the scars remained.

"Come to my place," Howard said. "It's not far from here, unless you want to stay in this bathroom all night."

She was thinking. Going to his place meant having sex. Did she want to have sex with him? Was there any reason not to have sex with him? She'd done much worse on impulse. He wasn't even a stranger, technically. He knew Greg. But why have sex with him?

He leaned back in and kissed her neck. "You smell good."

This close, he smelled pleasantly tangy from dried sweat and hair oil. She felt his warm breath on her skin. She liked men's bodies. They were interesting: the breadth of chest and arms, the hard span of them like the bridges and buildings they created in their likeness; their perpendicular rising, their horizontal dominance across the skin of the planet. So different from a woman. Being with a woman was to love a work of art in the flesh.

He released her, giving her space. He was not a stupid man. Maybe it came from his being mature. Young men so often pressure. She liked being touched; physical contact allowed her to feel. With women, she usually did the seducing. It was nice to be on the receiving end for a change.

"Okay. Sure."

He cautiously opened the door. Complete silence. "There's a back door," he said. "We'll go out that way."

She followed behind him, like "the little woman," and

snickered to herself.

"What?" he asked, turning and smiling at her. Then the lights in the club turned off. The door was right in front of them. He took her hand, pulling her out into the night.

THE HAPPY MEMORY

Six months later he took her to New Orleans. They woke in a heavily quilted bed with eyelet-covered pillows, in an antique brass four-poster. T.J. could smell French toast being made, the buttery, cinnamon and surgery smell coming from the kitchen in the B&B. She stretched and yawned. Howard's fingers curled into her hair. She looked at him and smiled.

"Good morning."

He raised himself up and pulled her to him.

"How about some boudoir cheesecake," he said, nibbling her ear.

"I have my period."

"So?"

"I don't want to mess up these lovely sheets. How about a blow job instead?" She slid down his body. He felt like the luckiest man alive. Of all the men and women in the world,

T.J. had chosen him.

They had lunch at Commander's Palace having agreed to spend a ridiculous amount of money on one great meal while they were in New Orleans. The waiter had recommended the turtle soup to start, a specialty of the house. It sounded terribly unappealing, and neither of them had ever had it, but the waiter smiled charmingly and said they wouldn't regret it.

"When in Rome..." Howard clinked T.J.'s glass of wine.

"When in Rome."

"This soup is extraordinary," T. J. exclaimed after every spoonful. "It's like someone turned velvet into liquid and created a new flavor that certainly wasn't turtle. I had turtles when I was a kid. Their bowls always stank even though I cleaned..."

"Let's not talk about turtle bowls while we are having this heavenly soup."

"Did you just use the word *heavenly*?"

"I did."

"You've never used that word."

He paused, spoon halfway to his mouth. "You're right. I probably haven't. But today, anything's possible. Like the deliciousness of turtle soup."

"If men's semen could taste like this, they would be getting blow jobs all the time from women all over the world."

He widened his eyes and raised his brows at her. "Are you saying that my own elixir of love could be improved upon?"

"What? No! I wouldn't trade your salty Jewish gefilte fish spunk for all the turtle soup in the world."

He laughed. He loved her.

She'd removed her shoe and ran her foot up his calf. He

grabbed her foot and put it in his lap so she could feel his hard-on. They moved their chairs closer. They ordered a second bottle of wine. Then they both ordered the Cornbread Crusted Des Allemands Catfish, seduced by the menu description: a sauté of Cajun andouille, grilled Vidalia onions, Louisiana red beans and roasted tomatoes with Creole tomato butter and smoked corn grits, and a side of wilted garlic spinach.

They took another swallow of wine and kissed. They giggled.

The food, the wine, their heat, the way T.J. was being her best, most affectionate self made Howard say words that he never thought would come out of his mouth. Never.

"T.J., will you marry me?"

She burst into a hearty, full-throated, laugh. Then she stopped and looked at him. "Yes."

He didn't know if she thought his proposal was a joke and that her answer was unserious, but he'd hold her to it. He looked at this delightful, girlish woman whose cheeks were the color of pink roses from the wine, and he thought, *I can die now. I've had this moment.*

After lunch they wandered across the street to the Lafayette Cemetery. There was no one there, just the two of them and the dead. They didn't talk. They held hands and silently read the inscriptions on ornate tombs and houses built above ground to keep loved ones safe from floating away. But there was no one home. The memories, the real remains of the dead, had vacated the property. What was left was human imagination making up ghost stories.

The monochrome grey of the day shrouded everything, threatening rain, making the place beautifully solemn and spooky. T.J. loved it.

They drifted apart and she took pictures that couldn't capture what she felt and saw, like catching light in your hand, turning evanescence into permanence, a trick to cheat time and death, like holding onto bones in graves.

There was a wisp of a tune in Howard's head, the bitter in the sweet, spirits incomprehensibly speaking in tongues as he tried to wrest meaning from the air. There was a lyric forming about a man who visits his best memory at a grave in the Lafayette Cemetery. His wife is still living, but the girl she once was is gone. It was his projection, of course. Too much happiness made him afraid.

He toyed with the title, "A Possible Ending."

He smirked. He was already expecting the worst. It came from being raised by a Jewish mother who doomed each piece of good news with forecasts of ruination. Near the end of her life, apropos of nothing, she looked at him from her bed and said, "You think anti-Semitism is over? Mark my words. It's just lurking below the surface. Don't be fooled. It will be back."

It began to drizzle, and Howard and T.J. sought each other out, realizing that this misting was starting to turn into real rain. They had no umbrella. Running, they left the graveyard and escaped into the first place of shelter, their hair and clothes wet and clinging.

The instant they walked in the door of the shop, they were assaulted by the smell of cat piss—like a hundred cat boxes needed cleaning. There was no one in sight, but after a moment the most welcoming man with a wonderful New Orleans accent, and clearly gay, appeared through a curtain from behind the counter.

"Mes Chers, come in out of the storm. Stay as long as you like. As you can see you are the only ones here. Forgive the cat stink. It gets worse in the damp. I have fifteen cats. But I love them all, and whenever another one shows up I can't turn it away."

He extravagantly opened his arms and gestured with both hands, "Come in, come in."

His blue and white striped sweater was rolled up at the sleeves, revealing heavy gold chain bracelets on each wrist. He had a waxed moustache that was very Dali-like and a most generous mouth that smiled as punctuation to every sentence.

"We're so sorry to be making puddles on your floor," T.J. said.

"Are you kidding? I am so used to puddles on the floor!"

T.J. laughed, and Howard grinned at this exuberant man who was graciously putting them at ease, even while their hair dripped and their skin felt clammy. If it weren't for that, Howard would be thinking about braving the downpour; the cat smell was that noxious to him. He looked out the opaque storefront windows sheeted in rain, a weak grey light giving the framed world a soft glow. The store definitely felt like a haven.

"You two are my new rescues. Please call me Albert."

Albert came from behind the counter to stand near Howard, extending his hand. "And you are?"

"Howard."

Albert met his eye as they shook hands.

"And I'm T.J."

Albert clasped her hand and held it cupped in his own. "We are kindred spirits. I can tell."

"I think you're right." T.J. smiled.

"Please," Albert said. "Look around. Don't worry about being wet. You can't hurt anything."

T.J. looked through the arch to the room on the right and saw flowers everywhere in all shapes and sizes, in pots, on pedestals, on shelves and the floor. She moved toward an impressive arrangement of orchids, but when she got close up she couldn't tell if they were real.

"May I?" she asked, looking back at Albert, her finger poised to touch.

"Of course," he nodded.

What she felt utterly astonished her. They were metal!

"They're enchanting! How is this possible? How do you do it?"

Albert was standing in the archway, beaming from the compliment.

Howard wasn't looking at the flowers. He was looking at T.J. in her delight. She was what he found enchanting. He came up behind her and whispered in her ear, "They're heavenly."

She turned her head toward him and breathed, "Yes." She kissed him on the cheek.

"Ah. You two are in love."

"Engaged," Howard said, "just today." He wondered if Albert had thought they were father and daughter when he first saw them.

"Then I must give you an engagement present!"

"Oh, no," T.J. said.

"But I insist! You've made my day."

She looked around excitedly, and of course she wanted the

grand, exquisite, large pieces, but she wouldn't ask for one of those. Instead, she went over to a small, perfect spray of pink flowers that she didn't know the name of, their delicate green stalks rising out of a small bed of rocks and earth. The flower's bell-shaped heads curved like ballerinas bowing. They were the most feminine things she'd ever seen.

"Can I have this one?"

"Of course! You must take it."

He plucked it off the shelf and put it in her hands, then walked back to the counter with T.J. following. She handed him the sculpture and he folded it in tissue paper and put it in a small paper bag with handles.

"You both must have lunch with me tomorrow at Commander's Palace. On me. I'm a regular there."

"Oh," T. J. said. "I wish we could."

"We leave tomorrow," Howard said.

"I wish we lived here and we could be best friends," T.J. said.

He smiled warmly at her. "But, we already are. You must promise to come back and see me again." He walked them to the door and handed T.J. his card.

"We'll call my invitation a rain check." He laughed. "Come whenever you need shelter from a storm."

The moist air seemed to hang in the doorway, without any real freshness to it, but Howard felt relief just inhaling.

The rain had stopped, but the heaviness remained, promising more of the same, and still they walked slowly down the empty, dripping streets, T.J. chattering all the way about Albert and his shop while holding onto Howard's arm, leaning into him. He was thinking how bewitched he was by this city, by this woman, and the sorcery of "Yes."

* * *

Thank you.

You're welcome, Howard.

Did we ever see Albert again?

No, I didn't.

What? You said I. I never saw him again.

Did I? I get very involved with my characters.

You're lying.

These days, I'm easily confused.

Why?

Must be the medications I'm on.

What? You take medications? What medications?

That's not relevant to the story, Howard.

I think it's relevant. What if you're really sick and you die before you finish this?

Yes. I do worry about that.

That's not reassuring.

I'm not going to die, Howard. I just worry about it. I've been worrying about it since I was five-years-old.

How can I believe you?

You just have to trust me.

The storyteller.

Right. I tell truth in fiction.

Is that like truth in advertising? This happened to you didn't it? This is your memory.

Changed. Disguised. Somewhat, but yes.

Do you still have it?

Have what?

Don't be coy.

Yes. I do still have it.

Where do you keep it?

The flowers are on a shelf facing my writing desk.

Is any of this fiction?

It depends on what you mean by fiction.

Oh, my God.

Can I get on with the story now, Howard?

I'm sort of really nervous about that.

* * *

Not even married a week and he hated to leave her for a gig in Ithaca, New York. He told her he would be gone three days, but he planned to be back after two to surprise her. It was only a four-hour drive, back by 4 a.m. Caffeine and thinking of her kept him awake. He imagined slipping into their bed and smelling her warm body as he lifted the sheets. Smell was very important. He once had a girlfriend who smelled acrid— like a panicked animal. He hated her odor, the stink of her sweat. It had nothing to do with being clean. T.J. could have not bathed for a month and he would still think she smelled wonderful. Smell was innate. Animal. You know you're with the wrong person if you hate their smell. He also loved T.J.'s musky essential oil that she bought from Keihl's on 13th street. Once, in an elevator, he got an erection from a woman standing near him. He was baffled. He hadn't even looked at her. Then he realized it was the scent she was wearing, a scent that might as well be called T.J.

He found a space on the street for the car, which was nothing short of a miracle. The luck of the newlywed. Of course, he would have to get up before 8 a.m. to move it to the other side of the street. Fucking Manhattan. In the afternoon he'd drive it back to his friend's house in Brooklyn where he could keep it parked in his garage. A pain in the ass, but at least it was free.

He'd moved into T.J.s loft on Broome Street—a gift from her parents after she graduated from N.Y.U.—because it only made sense. His place was a shoebox in the Village. The loft space was almost raw and it was a walk up. But he loved it. They had shoji screens that they moved around to create privacy. Unless they had company their bed was visible as soon as you opened the door to the loft. The bathroom had walls and a door. His drum kit sat in the living room/dining space. She'd had a dark room built when she'd moved in. The loft floor was concrete. He didn't know what the place had originally been used for—a sweatshop? Manufacturing? It had twenty-foot ceilings and a wall of windows. Heaven.

He took the stairs two steps at a time to the third floor, careful to tread lightly. He didn't want to wake her. He slowly turned his key in the deadbolt and quietly opened the door. Then stopped. They didn't have window coverings. The street light, their artificial moonlight, illuminated the bed in a dim, grey, night pall, making things ghostly. It wasn't just the two figures he saw in the bed—it was also the sounds that amplified across the empty space. First he made out the shape of the back of a body that looked like it could be an adolescent boy grinding into the pelvis of the figure underneath. That wasn't T.J.s ass. Not T.J.'s hair.

His core was melting down inside his burning skin. He felt nuclear.

T.J. opened her eyes when her partner stopped moving. They both stared at him as he stood next to the bed.

"Should I call the police?" the person on top asked. It was a woman.

"What the fuck is this?" He sounded to himself like he was talking through a breathing hole punched in his throat.

"I thought you wouldn't be home until tomorrow."

The young woman slid off T.J. and was sitting next to her, her legs curled under, incredibly calm as if this happened all the time.

T.J. raised herself up on her elbows. "Howard, this is Franny. I ran into her at a poetry reading tonight at the bookstore. Franny, this is Howard, my husband."

"We *just* got married!" Boom. He'd found his voice.

T.J. was sitting up now, the sheet around her waist. Neither of them seemed afraid or apologetic.

"Howard," T.J. said. "Come to bed. You must be tired." T. J. moved over to make room for him on her side of the bed.

His anger and sense of betrayal was switched in his brain to a different neural circuit. His delicious wife was offering sex with them both! Why was he getting angry? Wasn't this every man's dream? Isn't this what the bonobo apes do—calm the aggressive male by engulfing him and fucking his brains out?

He made monkey noises. T.J. laughed. He thumped his chest. Franny giggled. Then he slid over T.J's body and sandwiched himself between them. This was not the fantasy he'd had driving home. This was a different fantasy. Maybe even better.

That first year was a blizzard of good times that he was so caught up in, he failed to notice T.J. changing. She was very impressed with his famous friends. As a person who'd lived for years in the Village and hung out at bars and coffee houses, playing in the local clubs, going to the art-film houses and the downtown galleries, occasionally writing theater reviews covering the avant-garde and off Broadway—he knew a lot of people. He was genial and gregarious, an enthusiast. His being non-competitive and not particularly ambitious made him a welcome companion to all those striving, egomaniacal New Yorkers.

The parties and openings satisfied T.J.'s appetite to be around the famous and semi-famous, and she shot them all. In one year, her portfolio had grown considerably, and she imagined a show where the photos of prostitutes would be juxtaposed with photos of celebrities—six feet tall and in black and white.

"I'll call the show, 'The Art of Making Money.'"

"Too obvious," he'd said.

"You have a better name?" she'd fired back, annoyed.

"No."

Howard, in the meantime, loved being seen with her, loved watching her flirt, which gave him pleasure and turned him on. He didn't take the drugs she did because he didn't need an excuse to participate in group sex, or public sex, or a ménage a trois with T.J.

Then the sex began to dwindle. The gusher became a trickle and she started taking trips for her photography, trips he wasn't invited on. She complained that she had exhausted what she needed from NY and the southwest called to her, or the West Coast, or anywhere really that gave her an excuse to get away from him. The full realization of what was happening took about another year. Of course he was in denial. But then he hit on a solution.

"Let's have a baby."

T.J. looked at him like he had just proposed double suicide. She stopped chewing. They were having breakfast together on a Wednesday morning. T.J. had made his favorite breakfast, he supposed, as a conciliatory gesture for having been gone for six days.

A puckering between her eyebrows appeared—her distress signal. T.J.'s resistance was like a cat collapsing on the floor when you tried to leash-train it. You could drag it along the floor, saying, "Get up, get up," but the cat wouldn't budge. As soon as you removed the leash the cat sprang to its feet and fled. It was still in their early days and he was actually charmed by this. He had to sometimes suppress the laugh he felt because she would find it patronizing. When he used to laugh at her, she accused him of this. If he was being really honest with himself, he was probably threatened by this expression of hers. Whatever made him nervous made him laugh. Then again, he was so in love with her that everything charmed him: her breathing, snoring, scratching, moaning and the way she would sometimes look at him impressed and surprised. Her rare, open smile was the best.

* * *

Why am I so in love with her? I don't see anything lovable about her. How could she be the perfect woman I'd been wait-

ing for?

Maybe she was the imperfect woman you'd been waiting for. And maybe it has nothing to do with her, Howard. Maybe it's all about who you are.

Well, that pisses me off. I'm the good guy. I'm the injured party here.

Not now, Howard.

* * *

He knew she was screwing around, but he didn't talk about it. As long as she came back. He wanted to keep her. He never got tired of looking at her. Hers was a face that was endlessly interesting to him; not a perfect beauty, but from all angles she pleased him. The two dimples at the top of her ass cheeks just below the sway of her back were aesthetically sublime to him. Sometimes he would pretend to be reading and just watch her walk around the loft naked, as she paused by the window, staring out while sipping a cup of tea, or sitting and writing ideas in her notebook at her desk.

He admired her work. His friends liked her and were happy to make connections for her in the time-honored tradition of enamored older men helping the young and pretty get a leg up. This would usually require a trade for sexual favors. But T.J. knew how to keep herself pedestalled without being vulnerable, making it clear that she couldn't be touched. A staunch feminist was T.J., and mad to establish herself on her own merits, rationalizing the way she appealed to men and women, believing that there was no manipulation in it, no self-interest. He could say she married him for his connections, temporarily dazzled by the possibilities. Slowly, he began to see that she was losing interest. She had said she loved him and maybe she did. That didn't make it permanent. But he wanted the permanence. He actually liked how independent she was because it allowed him to maintain his former lifestyle except with the added benefit of her company. He didn't find her at all mysterious, but he did find her elusive, which kept him alert. She quivered, or lifted her head, or flared her nostrils, and he woke up. Was there some danger? Would she bolt?

No, he wasn't that jealous of her private affairs with women. It still allowed him to feel like he was the man in her life.

* * *

I'm a putz. Or a masochist.
You're a man in love. And you're an unconventional man.
I don't like myself.
That's part of it, isn't it, Howard?

* * *

"I want us to have a child," he said, ignoring her warning. He wasn't looking at her; he was looking at his half-finished pancake sitting in a pool of syrup. If he made eye contact she might feel threatened.

"No."

"Why not?"

"Because I don't want children."

"Why not?"

He broke off a bite of pancake and swirled it in the syrup then popped it in his mouth, acting like he was only vaguely interested in this conversation.

"I have no interest in children. I have no interest in taking care of a child."

"But I do. I could."

"Look at me, Howard."

He looked at her and as soon as he did he couldn't disguise his affection. With T.J. he didn't hide his feelings. Maybe he should have, maybe she was losing respect for him because she could push him around.

"You have to work. It would be expensive."

Her voice was cold. A line drawn in the sand, but then she surprised him. When he didn't argue back she reached over and cupped his face in her hand and smiled at him, one of those acknowledging smiles, taking him in. This was her thank you.

He dropped it.

Six months later, as they lay in bed in the half dark with her head resting on his chest, he caressed her hair and whispered, "Let's have a child," kissing the top of her head. He paused and kept caressing. She didn't stir, didn't say anything.

"I'll do all the parenting. You won't have to do a thing past pregnancy and birth."

She sighed.

Was that a sigh of resignation? he thought hopefully. But then she said, "That is so weird. Why do you want a child?"

"I'm nesting? Being married to you makes me want a baby, too. A wife and child."

"This is so not who I thought you were. This is very disappointing. This is a total role reversal. You're like a woman with a penis."

"If I were a man with a womb we wouldn't be having this conversation."

She rolled off his chest and propped herself up on one arm and looked at him.

"Okay. I want a child because it would be us. A part of you and a part of me. A blending."

"You want to anchor me."

"No, I want to free you, but I won't be alone. I will still have you in a sense." And you'll come back, he thought. The tie that binds.

"You wouldn't expect anything from me?"

"Nothing. Our daughter. My responsibility."

"How do you know it will be a girl?"

"Because I want a girl, so I may as well believe that is what we'll have."

"I'll think about it."

Ten months later, she gave him a baby girl.

"It was my idea. I want to name her."

As T.J. held the baby in her arms in the hospital and looked down at her, she said, "Sinclair."

"Why Sinclair?" He hoped to call her Brett because he always liked that name ever since he read Hemingway's *The Sun Also Rises*.

"I just like it."

"Too formal for a baby."

"But a fabulous name for a grown female." She grinned at him.

"Then let me give her a middle name. I want to name her

after my mother, Rose."

T.J. considered, then nodded.

He put his finger on the soft baby skin and repeated, "Sinclair. Little Sinclair Rose."

True to her word, T.J. never changed a diaper or responded to Sinclair's cries. He was the one who got up at night and attended to the baby, fed her the pumped milk from T.J's breasts, took her to the doctor, and entertained her, buying toys, playing peek-a-boo, making up stories. He was so in love with this child. He didn't mind when T.J. left town, or that she had no maternal interest in the baby. He felt bad for Sinclair, but he compensated by being both mother and father to her. He was lucky to have a flexible, freelance career. He stepped up the writing and pretty much suspended playing out until Sinclair was old enough to bring with him. Fortunately, T.J. was starting to make money. She was picked up by a gallery in New York and another in L.A. She was selling well enough that, between their two incomes, they could survive.

Then, when Sinclair was nine, out of the blue, T.J. noticed her. Suddenly she took an interest. Sinclair immediately responded. Rather than mistrusting her mother or holding her former disinterest and absence against her, Sinclair fell madly in love with T.J. Just like that Sinclair pretty much dropped Howard. T.J. was the one fascinating her, making her laugh, and having private conversations. No Boys Allowed. No Daddies.

To say that he was hurt was beyond an understatement. It utterly baffled him.

"Why now, T.J.?"

"I don't know. Maybe because she can walk and talk and

has a brain that interests me. I told you I don't like babies. Now we can have conversations. I can teach her things."

And she had a new photographic subject. She documented Sinclair and herself. Naked portraits of mother and daughter in staged, "candid" moments of relationship, expressing all the emotions that Howard never witnessed in T.J. were nakedly expressed in all their moving complexity. There was nothing sentimental in these portraits. They ran the gamut from tender attachment, to objectification of their twin selves, and emotional bondage. She merged them and separated them, and catalogued both of them changing over several years. When Sinclair turned thirteen, however, the photographing stopped. T.J.'s shows were all sold and she was getting interviews. A coffee table book was in progress.

* * *

So, this is just great. I'm now fifty-one with a thirteen-year-old-daughter and a gay wife who has marginalized me.

They still love you, Howard. It's just a phase.

I don't feel loved. I feel used.

Why don't you get into therapy?

Do I have a choice?

Not really.

* * *

Howard went to see Dr. Glick on 12th Street right across from The New School. He had a small, nondescript office that thankfully wasn't cluttered with African masks or *The Scream* by Munch. It was functional and comfortable: two stuffed easy chairs of some forgettable color and fabric faced each other over a brown coffee table that had a box of tissues on it. The beige blinds were drawn. A small desk behind Dr. Glick's chair was cleared of any personal items or paperwork, just some books propped between two bronze hands. A standing lamp created all the necessary light. He liked the office. It was worn and unintimidating, like Dr. Glick, who was a droopy faced, middle-aged gentleman, with bushy brows that were starting to grey. He had a solid Germanic nose, which was his boldest feature and took up a substantial part of his face. His bushy moustache matched his brows. His lips were unusually red, with the upper lip disappearing into the moustache. The prominent lower lip was wide, large and soft. The sharpest thing about his features were his dark brown eyes, alive with an intelligence that did as much commenting and "talking" as anything that came out of his mouth. Howard thought of them as the Greek chorus of their conversation.

"The question is not why does she stay with you, but why do you stay with her, Howard?"

"I don't know, Doc." Howard was looking at his hands in his lap. He once thought he had fine hands, Michelangelo worthy, with a particular masculine beauty. Someone once told him he could have been a hand model. Now he saw the veins and the network of fine lines everywhere that one day would crepe and wrinkle like his father's hands. T.J. wouldn't let these hands touch her anymore.

"Try to explain."

"She doesn't bore me."

"And what else?"

Dr. Glick had a pipe stuck in his mouth that he didn't light. Howard liked the sound of the click his teeth made on the wooden stem when he would remove the pipe to talk, or bite on it when he put it back in. Maybe Howard should get a pipe. It was such a comforting, masculine prop. It communicated a kind, professorial authority. Howard would like some calm authority to leaven his internal rage.

"The thing is, Doc, I don't see the point in making a change. I'm going to die, and the longer I live the more I realize that fact. I may as well stay with T.J. because I have no desire to go out and find someone else, or do anything different, for that matter."

"You're right, Howard. We all die. So the only thing that does matter is giving each moment of our life personal meaning. We are the creators of our lives. Since it's all random, and without design, we are free. The tragedy then would be to squander every minute because the present is all we have."

"It doesn't make me feel that way. I don't think we're free. We're trapped by economics, by culture, by a deluded government. But, I'm not saying you're wrong. T.J. tells me to travel. To go visit relatives in Europe. But I don't want to. The thought of packing and getting on a plane makes me anxious. Anything outside my routine feels like a burden."

"That's because you're depressed. Perhaps if you changed your routine, even in a minor way, you would get some relief. Crack a window, Howard."

This conversation was making him feel worse. He just wanted sympathy. He wanted to complain. He didn't want solutions or to be told to "seize the day" and live in the present. He wanted respect for getting old and being cranky about it, and to be told that it was okay to feel diminished and to fear dying.

"Howard, you're only fifty-one. You may have a right to say these things at seventy-one. Let's get back to T.J.," Dr. Glick said. "Tell me about your relationship with her now."

He didn't want to think about it. He didn't want to talk about their last fight.

After Sinclair was born they built a room for her, but sound carried like crazy in the loft and Rosie—the name he called her—grew up hearing everything. He hoped she escaped under her headphones. T.J. was a screamer, and when provoked, so was he.

T.J. had just come back from a shoot in Arizona, but she had really gone there because of Cherie, her girlfriend. T.J. told him she was in love.

"I think you should move out," she said as soon as she walked in, flinging her keys on the table in the hall.

"What? You're crazy! Why would I move out?" He was in bed and had been reading a book on Brecht. Sinclair was presumably asleep. Or had been. T.J. was making no effort to keep her voice down.

"I want Cherie to move in with me."

Cherie was ten years younger than T.J. What was remarkable to him was that no matter what age T.J. became, she remained a sexual magnet. She was an erotic creature. She had sexual charisma. Not charm. She wasn't charming. She was without the civilizing veneer of inhibitions, or the female self-hate promoted by culture. Every woman he'd ever known, no matter how beautiful, always asked, "How do I look?" Every one of them hated some physical part of themselves. But not

T. J. She never asked because she didn't care. She wasn't in the least bit vain. She wasn't a woman who spent time in front of a mirror, despite the fact that her professional life depended on the visual judgments and calculations of her eye and brain. The naked photos of her and Sinclair were never about how she looked as an object of desire. Nor was it Marie Cassatt as photographer celebrating the beautiful intimate moments of motherhood. Some of the photos reminded him of nature photography where you see the human in the animal eyes of a resting lioness and her cub. There was a shot of the two of them, teeth bared, facing off against each other, Sinclair's long hair lifted in the air in still motion, like the hair on a cat's humped back raised in threat. T.J's. head is a double exposure, one face with teeth bared snarling back and the other looking away, either refusing to see or utterly indifferent. Sinclair hated this photo. It made her feel the anger that she hadn't felt during the shot, which was entirely staged by T.J.

Women usually loved her work. Many men found it disturbing. It's hard as a man to see a woman's naked body as maternal and separate from the desirable. The distancing necessary for men to be sexual, to not see vaginas and bellies and the open space between a woman's legs as their original home, as the space where their infant heads once appeared, meant that they have to objectify it. She is not my mother. Even though she has a body like my mother's body, she is not her. You'd think that being born from women would create lifelong awe and respect. Instead it too often resulted in fear and loathing. He believed he felt all of it.

"I'm not leaving T.J. This is my home, too. That's my daughter. If Cherie moves in and I move out, who will take care of Sinclair?"

"I will. Or Cherie will."

"That's my point exactly. You may like to play with your doll child, but you *don't* take care of her."

"Well, she's thirteen now. She isn't a child anymore."

"That's typical. I guess you could marry her off to some oil sheik since she's all grown up, and you and Cherie could have the place to yourselves."

"AAAAAAAHHHHHH!!! I am so trapped!"

Howard smiled. "That's absurd. You have the freedom most people would envy."

"But THIS is not what I want!"

"It won't last with Cherie, T.J. It never does."

She took off a boot and threw it at him. He ducked.

She stomped around the loft, peeling her clothes off, fuming.

He was so angry about this constant replay in their lives. *He* was the one who was trapped because he loved Rosie and he still loved T.J. In the past, he had slept with every woman that responded to him. He loved sex. He loved women. But he never fell in love with a woman, not until T.J.

He watched her talking bitterly to herself, punching the air, and pacing back-and-forth until she had exhausted herself. He greedily looked at her body. She was desire personified to him. He hated himself for his erection. He had learned "you can look, but you can't touch."

T.J. went into the kitchen, got a wine glass, opened a bottle of red and poured herself a full glass. She gulped it down. She poured another and drank a bit more slowly. Finished, she stuck a stopper in and put it in the fridge, placed the glass in the sink, and calmly crossed the room and got into bed next to him.

He turned off the bedside lamp, put his book on the floor and slid under the covers. "T.J.," he whispered from his side of the bed. "Can we have sex?"

She didn't look at him. "Yes."

She pulled the covers off her and began caressing her breasts as he watched, stroking himself. She kept one hand on her breast, playing with her nipple, while her other hand slipped between her open legs and she began masturbating. As her rhythm and breath grew more excited, so did he. His goal was always to come with her, to read her sounds and body to know when she was about to orgasm so he could, too. It was the best he could hope for, all she would allow, and he was grateful for even this. But he also hated her.

"Why don't you take lovers, Howard?" Dr. Glick asked.

"T.J. asks me the same thing. I don't want to. Look Doc, I met T.J. when I was almost forty. She was twenty-three. Before that I'd been with many, many women. What can I say? When we were dating, it was only me and T.J. I loved our sex life. After I married T.J. we had a wild sex life. It was the culmination of all my sexual fantasies and I was doing it all with the woman I loved. After T.J. lost interest in me, except for the occasional pity fuck, and then with the birth of Sinclair, I turned some kind of corner. It wasn't like one day I was a lusty male heterosexual and the next day I was utterly neutered; I still had appetites, desires, but they were all for T.J. The more unavailable she became, the more I yearned for her. In time it got to be a habit, I suppose. To this day, T.J. turns me on. I'm like an addict in my single-minded devotion to only one drug."

* * *

Who the fuck is T.J.? I'm not getting her. She's not a real character. She's like an idea, a foil that is being used to describe me.

Okay, Howard. Let's see what I can do to help.

* * *

The baby was wailing, waking T.J. up from her character-istic deep sleep. Her gut twisted. Howard was already up. She felt the side of his bed. Still warm. She rolled away on her other side feeling guilty and angry. He'd been true to his word. He did all the caretaking. He made it all sound like it would be so easy for her. Nothing about it was easy for her, not the preg-nancy, not the delivery, and certainly not her mood. More than ever she wanted to run away. The child was this unfathomable sack of need. She could look at her when she was asleep. But awake and animated, T.J. wanted to skulk off. How could she have let Howard talk her into this? Howard never complained. He was in love. A love that was covered in spit up and baby poop and breast milk. She was now an outsider in her own home. When she was pregnant she felt inhabited by an alien. He talked her out of an abortion. She went through with their bargain. And now that Sinclair was here she felt like a freak of nature; she felt inhuman not to have bonded, not to feel ten-derness and love. She was depressed. Deeply depressed. How-ard said it was normal. Postpartum depression. It would pass. He talked like it was a bad case of gas. It would pass. His relentless cheerfulness, his grinning adoration made her feel like a monster, particularly because it made her want to kill him. She'd promised she would stick around, not make plans for trips for the first six months while she pumped and he fed Sinclair her breast milk. She knew he'd thought she'd come around, that the primal tide of nature, the strong undertow of maternal love would grab her and sweep her emotionally away. How could she not love her own daughter?

She rolled on her other side, wishing for sleep. She wanted a sleeping pill or a bottle of wine, but Howard wouldn't allow it. Not good for the baby. A tear dripped onto the pillow. She closed her eyes. She often dreamt about Sinclair. The same dream in different guises. She was sitting at the kitchen table at her parents' house. There was a party going on. All her parents' friends were drunk and laughing, carrying on. In front of her on the kitchen table was an infant in a carrier swaddled in a pink blanket. The baby wasn't crying or moving. The baby wasn't making a sound. It was turning blue. She was expecting one of the adults to notice, to help the baby, but they'd just stagger by, not seeing her or the dying infant. She wanted to scream, Help! Help! She wanted to shake them. But she knew it would be useless. They wouldn't be competent to do a thing. She also knew that this baby was hers. The baby had been neglected, not fed, put away in a drawer until she found it in dirty unchanged diapers. She was appalled at herself. How could she not know she'd had a baby?! She couldn't touch the child. She needed help. She didn't have any idea what to do. She was terribly, terribly frightened. And now the baby would die because there were no grownups to take care of it.

That nightmare shook her awake on too many nights to

count, anguished and gasping for air.

* * *

I can't stand this. This is appalling. This is my wife? The woman I fell in love with? What woman feels this way? You should be the one in therapy. You know, there are plenty of writers who write about things other than themselves.

I don't believe that. Characters are personas, avatars. The brain is a curator, a biased consciousness. History is not objective, human truth is not objective. You just don't like my story, Howard, because it's dark and without heroes. Maybe you dislike everyone in it, including yourself. But I have great sympathy for all of you. Tragedy and human shortcomings, the myth of what we should be, our struggle with that, touches me. Makes me want to weep.

Makes me want to rend my flesh.

Me too, Howard. Me too.

Wait a minute, in the beginning, when you were getting me out of bed, you said, I had to be named Howard because you'd already made Howard famous.

Joke.

Joke's on me then.

No, Howard, the joke's really on me.

That, what you just said, that's really funny.

Howard, look, this is how it works. Think about the Genesis story: Adam made out of dust? Eve from a rib? Magic realism? Fantasy fiction? Dystopian future? Is God the author of the world? Or was it those men who were actually artists who believed they were writing down the truth, transcribing stories from the past, from eyewitnesses long since dead. It's like the game, Telephone. One child tells another child a story and the next repeats it, until you have the last child tell the story out loud, and now it's about a man who is the son of God and can change water into wine, and rise from the dead. Amazing. It's the western world's original piece of fiction, a bestseller for centuries because it's a story we tell ourselves about ourselves. Our human nature has never changed—so colorful, and nuts, and full of cautionary tales, and contradictions, and violence, and aspiration—therefore it's a story that still appeals to us. Fiction turned real through belief.

You don't believe we're real do you?

No, no, of course not. Enough chitchat. Maybe this will give you some sympathy for your wife.

* * *

T.J. escaped to the museums whenever she could, the one place she came alive. She'd stopped photographing. Howard said it was temporary, but he couldn't know. At the Met, when she entered a room her eyes scanned the walls of paintings looking for the one or two that excited her. These she saved like dessert, spending the rest of the time anticipating. Finally, when she walked up to the one she'd been saving for last, she surrendered to it, losing herself in the sheen of pearls, light shading a wall, the pop of yellow from a fallen petal; she ached to touch those silvered silks or that bit of cuff lace. What was this elation, why was it caused by these perfect shades of red, these satin blues? Her brain analyzed, but couldn't fathom the immediacy of her sensual response. The people, the faces, could pierce her with tenderness, make her spill tears, or make her want to kiss lips, and know stories. Their stories were paused, as if they were Sleeping Beauty waiting for the right gaze to make them move again. There were so many paintings she wanted to enter, to walk toward their different horizons. Some paintings she sat in front of for an hour or more. If she could suck them into herself so that they became a part of her, she could leave the museum stuffed, finally filled, and satisfied.

Fortunately, there were also paintings that brought her peace, allowing her to transcend herself, her brain chatter quieted. It was the arts, not religion that were holy to her. The masters, the standard bearers, the benchmark setters, that she could never get close to in her own art. But that didn't matter. All that mattered was that they existed as an alternative testimony to all the grasping, violent, selfish things about humanity. She would leave the museum burned clean. She would walk around the city not seeing anything. She remained lifted, in this state of grace. This was her blood infusion for the day, the kiss of life, which allowed her to go back home to Howard and Sinclair instead of walking in front of a bus.

* * *

See, this is what I love her for, what I admired. That's what we had in the beginning, this bond over music and art. We talked endlessly about both. I was teaching her to see through my eyes as much as she was letting me see through hers. But I didn't know she was that depressed.

Why didn't you know, Howard?

Because all that mattered then was my baby, Sinclair Rose. I felt like I was living alone with my daughter, who needed me. T.J. had checked out.

You were angry.

A part of me wanted it different, secretly hoped it might be. But I also liked having full control, making all the decisions, having her all to myself, exhausting as it was. I was so in love with my child.

Clearly, T.J. was angry.

I see that now. But not about the baby, not about losing me to Sinclair. She just didn't have the life she wanted.

Maybe.

You mean I'm wrong?

Do you really think that dream T.J. had was about Sinclair? Who was the dying baby that the inept grownups ignored?

I hadn't considered that. She's the frightened mother and the dying child? Am I all the oblivious grownups?

Another part of herself.

So the dreamer is all the characters, and the author is all the characters?

Right.

You do know you're talking to yourself?

You're very real to me, Howard. These conversations with you are very helpful.

Wait. You know something I just realized? I don't know where Sinclair is. She wasn't home all night. What have you done to my daughter?! This is scaring me. I don't know where this is going.

That's exactly my fear. I also don't know where this is go-

ing.

Why can't you be one of those writers that make a plan?

Because that's not how I write. It's not even how I live. We all make plans, Howard, but we have no control over the outcomes. Writing is the only control I have.

That's what you believe?

Yes.

But you're out of control here.

That's true. Maybe you should offer me a human sacrifice, Howard, so I can figure out the next part. You know, being that I am your God.

You are not taking my daughter!

I haven't decided.

YOU are NOT taking my daughter!

You know, historically, millions of children were lucky to survive to fourteen.

Healthy American children make it to ninety-five today.

Okay, Howard. No human sacrifice. I was just toying with the idea. Which would make the story better.

Death is not the answer.

Okay, I will live.

I thought we were talking about Sinclair?

Of course we were, Howard.

You said, I.

☺

* * *

Sinclair held onto the subway pole, legs wide to keep her balance on the lurching train. She tried to shed her resentment about living in Englewood, New Jersey when Manhattan used to be at her doorstep. T.J. had lied. She didn't move them because she wanted to retreat from the art scene and the bullshit, she wanted to live closer to her girlfriend. Her money, her rules. Poor Howard. Of course he acquiesced to everything. Her heart fisted just thinking about him, the rush of scorn and contempt conflicted with her youngest and deepest feelings of loving her daddy. It was all layered in there, impossible to think about, so she shut it down.

Her eye was caught by a guy who she realized was staring at her. Before she saw the penis in his hand she felt his creepiness, her stomach clenching as her flesh prickled from her scalp down to the back of her neck and arms. She looked away and walked toward the door that connected the cars, praying that he wouldn't follow her. Why was she stupidly standing in an empty car? She hoped to God she would find people in the next one.

Empty. She moved swiftly through this car, her heart hammering, afraid to look back, and then, finally, in the next car there was a middle-aged woman reading a book with a lurid cover and a man in a coat and tie doing a crossword puzzle. She quickly glanced back at the connecting door. He wasn't there. She shivered just thinking about him. Feeling safer, her heart calmed down. Only two more stops.

She adjusted her very large bag on her shoulder to stop the strap from digging into it. She may be fifteen but she looked at least seventeen, or even eighteen. It was because of how tall she was and all that basketball practice gave her muscles that matured her body. She probably hadn't even reached her full height yet. She was five feet, ten and a half inches.

Pretty much a freak.

Sinclair got out at Houston Street and stood on the corner looking at the address on the paper again. She was looking for the loft studio where the art class was being held. She re-read the name of the guy she'd met at the 8th Street Bookstore last week. He was in an office at the back stocking books and she'd stood in the doorframe to ask him a question about a poster she couldn't find. When he looked up he'd stared at her before responding. It was weird. He told her they were sold out. She thanked him and walked away, but he followed and caught up to her in the middle of the store.

"Excuse me."

She turned around.

"Yes?"

"I was wondering, would you like to make some money?"

That surprised her. "Doing what?"

"I'm part of a group of visual artists that meet privately for a drawing class and we're always looking for models."

She instantly felt flattered and also experienced the fear and excitement that accompanied anything new, something she would have to keep secret and made her feel mildly out-of-control.

"What do I have to do?"

He was already fishing the pen from his shirt pocket and pulling a small spiral notepad from his back pocket. Flipping it open, he wrote something, tore the paper from the pad, and handed her the address with his name on it. Richard Bogen.

"What do I have to do?"

"Just stand there and let about five or six of us draw you. The class is two hours. You get breaks. And you get paid twenty dollars per hour."

She folded the paper into her pocket.

"The class is this Friday night at 7:00. Will you come?"

His complete attention was fixed on her so that she felt pressured to say something. Customers were asking him questions, but he ignored them. The tension inside her was getting unbearable.

"Okay, yes."

Then he gave her a slight smile, nodded, and got swallowed up in the clamor of customers. She walked out of the bookstore.

Did that really just happen? The brisk, fall air made walking fast a pleasure. She pictured what he looked like and the sequence of events, but the harder she focused, the more the details disappeared. What color was his hair? What was he wearing? The only vivid thing she remembered was his eyes boring into her. Twenty dollars an hour! She wanted to break into a run.

She stood in front of a four-story building on Spring Street, old red brick with a zigzagging fire escape. There were lights shining from the third floor. She pressed the apartment number listed on the paper. In a moment the front door buzzed and she pushed it open and went in. The hall was dimly lit, filled with stagnant cold air that smelled like decaying newspapers and mouse droppings. She saw newsprint stuffed between exposed beams as a makeshift way to keep drafts out. In front of her was a staircase and on the right was a freight elevator. Just entering the building had scared her. Now, even more scared, she hesitated, arguing with herself, then chose the steps.

At the third landing there was a green door with the number 301 on it. She knocked. No answer. What a stupid mistake she'd made. Then the door opened. There was Richard Bogen in a black turtleneck and jeans, looking as she remembered him. Intense. Weird. He gave her an acknowledging nod and waved her in, stepping out of her way. Then he closed and locked the door. The large, open space was very brightly lit. There was a circle of chairs and easels. A handful of men were talking at a refreshment table that had a coffee pot, mugs, and two plates of donuts. At the center of the circle was a chair, a full length mirror, and a space heater. To the left of the circle was a six-foot-tall folding screen that looked like something she'd seen in old movies in actress's dressing rooms. It had some faded pink and green landscape silk-screened on it. A folded white bath towel hung over the top.

She walked over to the coffee and donuts and poured herself a cup. Everyone there looked like a college student or a bit older. Richard Bogen was in the older camp. Maybe even twenty-five or twenty-six? She was in over her head, but the vibe of the room was not menacing. It was like a club meeting.

"You must be the new model," the guy beside her said, a tall blonde with dangling curls that almost fell into his eyes. He gave her a friendly smile. "Don't worry about us. You'll get used to our staring at you and then you won't even notice we're doing it. Then you'll get bored."

She nodded her head, unwilling to admit this was her first time. She didn't want to seem like a baby.

Richard Bogen was clapping his hands and saying, "Okay, everyone, it's time to start." She glanced at her wrist watch. 7:10 p.m.

Bogen was at her side, ushering her to the screen. "Get undressed and wrap yourself in the towel if you like. Then take the seat in the middle. You can put the towel on the chair and sit on it. Believe me, after posing for a while on a hard stool, you'll appreciate the padding. Tell me if the space heater is too hot or not hot enough. I can always reposition it."

"I didn't know I would have to get undressed."

He smiled. "Believe me, it's not at all sexual. Your body is no different to us than a bowl of fruit. We just need a body to draw. Any body. But many people are too self-conscious to do this. You strike me as a girl that's pretty game for anything."

Again, she felt flattered.

"Trust me, you'll get the hang of this in no time."

"You didn't explain this. I just didn't know."

"It didn't occur to you that that was why we were paying twenty an hour?"

"I didn't think."

"Well, you're here now, so get undressed. Everyone is expecting to draw tonight, and you're it."

He took her by her shoulders and gently pushed her behind the screen. "Do it quickly. In two hours you'll be forty dollars richer. Focus on that."

She thought, *what the fuck*, and stripped off her clothes. Life is about taking risks and having adventures, isn't it? This would be one of many, many firsts. *She* was not going to settle down in Englewood, New Jersey, and become a boring suburban teenager. You can take the girl out of the city, but you couldn't take the city out of the girl. This was her life. Screw her mother.

She stepped out with the towel wrapped around her and

kept her eyes pretty much on her bare feet as she walked toward the chair, removed the towel, and folded it on the seat as instructed. She had been cold until she was sitting right in front of the heater.

"Just sit in a position that is comfortable to you," Bogen said. "You're going to have to hold it for ten minutes. Then we'll take a five-minute break and let you move and relax. Since this is your first time we'll take more breaks than usual. Until then, hold perfectly still."

She still hadn't looked up. She decided she would continue for as long as she needed to. She could do this.

"Okay, we're starting now. I'll tell you when ten minutes are up. I'll give a two-minute warning so the artists know to wrap it up."

She sat with her legs crossed, her back rounded, one arm draped over her knee, and the other arm loosely hanging beside her. After what was probably only a couple of minutes, she desperately wanted to move. Her nose itched and she wanted to rub it, and now couldn't think of anything else but. She wanted to uncross and re-cross her legs, switching sides. She had never been so conscious of her body. The lack of permission to move made it the only thing she wanted. She was afraid to raise her eyes to look around. What if someone was drawing them and she'd ruin it? More itches. The space heater was too hot on her legs with not enough warmth getting to her back and shoulders. She wanted to ask for it to be repositioned but she was afraid to speak. What if someone was drawing her lips?

You can do this became her mantra. *You can do this*. Only ten minutes. How many had passed? She thought maybe her leg supporting her crossed leg was falling asleep.

"Two more minutes," she heard Bogen say.

Thank you, Jesus. The two minutes passed like ten. How long can a minute take?!

"Take a break, Sinclair." Five minutes.

She uncrossed her legs, stretched her back and stood. Ahhh. She picked up the towel and wrapped it around herself and made a beeline for the coffee and donuts. Most of the artists stayed at their easels and continued working. If the ten minutes was that hard, how was she going to get through the evening? She couldn't make eye contact with anyone. Fortunately, no one tried to speak to her.

Then Bogen was by her side. "Trust me, it gets easier."

She looked at him. It was weird to be standing next to an older guy with only a towel on. No one had ogled her. She was a plant, a potato, a set of geometric shapes. It was totally unsexy, which she was grateful for.

"I'm okay," she said. "Piece of cake."

"Really? Then you'd be okay sitting for a twenty-minute stretch?"

"Um, well, maybe not yet."

He smirked. "That's okay. First time. You've gotta learn some tricks. Practice at home in front of a mirror doing poses that you can hold. Time yourself. Use your hands and feet. Think of yourself as expressive from the feet up. Find a spot to focus on. Meditate, if you can. You know, if you get good at this, you can make as much as fifty an hour."

Wow, she thought, nodding. She wondered if he had any idea of how old she was? She glanced at him. They were about the same height. He was pouring coffee for himself.

He was about to take a sip when he added, "Bring a bath-robe next time. Wash the towel and bathrobe between sessions. Before you come, take a shower and moisturize yourself."

He looked at her. "You have great skin, but you don't want any dry patches. They are drawing the texture and light and shadow. We want the skin smooth everywhere. Soles of your feet, even."

She nodded again, taking a bite of donut.

"Okay, let's get started. Ten minutes."

When the agonizing two hours were up, Bogen asked her to stay a moment to pay her. She went behind the screen and put her clothes back on. By the time she'd finished dressing, everyone else had left.

"You did good. For a first timer."

He grinned. And then he just stood there looking at her, making her uncomfortable. His eyes had changed, like in the bookstore. He was normal in the stockroom when she poked her head in to ask her question, but when he came after her he was different, like now. That focused gaze that felt like he was trying to control her. It was safe in the bookstore, but here it was creepy.

"My money?" she said, acting like she hadn't noticed the shift in him. He didn't answer; he didn't move. He just stared.

"Forty bucks, you said. Twenty an hour." Could he tell she was nervous?

This is how it works, she thought. He lures young women here and everything is normal. Until he's alone with you. And then it's not.

Saying nothing, his hand reached for her.

She turned and started to run, but he was just as fast and grabbed her arm. She heard her father's voice in her head. "Sinclair, turn around and kick him in the nuts!"

She stunned them both by the ferocity of that kick. Bogen doubled over, clutching his groin and groaning. She rushed to the door and pulled hard on the handle. Locked. She glanced back and saw Bogen regaining his balance—an appalling glimpse of scarlet face and open mouth. The deadbolt was hard to twist. She heard his frightening sounds coming from behind her. Pumped full of adrenaline, commanding both hands to work faster, the knob turned and she yanked the door open.

"You cunt! Bitch! Don't you ever fucking come back here!"

She looked up from the second stair landing and saw his twisted face leaning over the railing. "Whore!" He flung her money after her.

She reached the bottom and looked back up for the last time. He was gone. The money had fallen down the shaft between the stairs and the elevator. She scooped up the two twenties and ran out the front door and into the night.

* * *

See, Howard? I didn't kill her.

No, but you're fucked up. Doing that to my daughter.

I was someone's daughter, Howard.

What are you talking about? This happened to you?

Not in this exact scenario, but yes. A famous children's author who was thirty years older than me invited me to his apartment to listen to his jazz collection. He was a friend of a family friend, so I figured it was okay. Once we were in his apartment, he made selections from his albums that lined the walls. As we listened, he educated me. I was appropriately impressed, and quite enjoying myself. I loved talking with him. I had no clue that this was some timeworn performance, a theatrical trick to make himself desirable. Brains and fame, the gateway drug to sex.

Then, obeying some internal signal that let him know the chitchat was over, he moved closer to me on the couch and pulled me to him, smashed my lips with his, and tried to thrust his tongue in my mouth.

Ugh! He'd instantly become this bald, gnarly, leathery thing that was touching me!

"NO!!!" I shouted.

His shocked look of disbelief, his "Who The Fuck Do You Think You Are?!" was so astonishing to me that at first I couldn't move. He screamed at me again, "Get out, you stupid cunt!"

Then I bolted. Running down the stairs, I heard those very words that Sinclair heard, and worse.

That's incredible.

This sort of thing happens a lot to girls and young women.

That can't be true.

It is, Howard. You don't know this because you're a man. A white man.

You're exaggerating.

Am I?

* * *

Back to the beginning...

"Sinclair? Sinclair, get down here. Breakfast."

A few minutes later, Howard went to the foot of the stairs. "Sinclair!" He didn't give a shit if he woke T.J.

No answer. He started up the stairs, getting more annoyed at each step. He didn't want breakfast to be ruined. He knocked on her door. Still no answer. "Sinclair?" He opened it. Empty, bed still made, unslept in. Panic set in.

"T.J." he roared, running down the hall to their bedroom.

"What *is* it, Howard? Why are you screaming at me?" She pushed her eye mask onto her forehead and looked at him, annoyed, until she saw his face. He strode up to the bed, "Sinclair is gone. She hasn't been home all night!"

"What?"

"Where could she be?"

T.J., fully awake, was slipping a t-shirt over her head that she'd left on the floor beside the bed along with a pair of sweatpants.

"This is your fault, T.J."

"What the hell does that mean, Howard?"

Howard was pacing.

"It was you who moved us out here. We were fine in NY. Sinclair loved our loft. She loved living in the city. We were happy there."

"I wasn't happy there, Howard."

"Screw you. Screw your girlfriend."

"Howard, you better calm down."

"You get everything, T.J.—a daughter, a caretaker, a career, lovers..."

"You can have lovers. I've told you many times you should

get a lover."

"Permission from T.J.! If I wanted lovers, I'd have them."

"So, what's stopping you?"

"You, you smug..." He almost said it, almost called her a bitch, but he caught himself. He promised himself no more tirades, no more cursing her, and it wasn't her fault. It was his. He stayed. He put up with it. She paid the bills. He was utterly financially dependent now.

Then Sinclair appeared in the bedroom doorframe. She looked really upset. "I'm sorry."

"You're sorry?! Where the hell have you been!" He started toward her threateningly, but she ran. He chased her through the house until he cornered her in the bathroom and slapped her across the face, then turned around and left.

When he slapped her all she could feel was an explosion of pain. She thought maybe her nose was broken. But it was more than that. It was like her mind disconnected from her body for that instant. Time and reality had been slapped. He'd never hit her before.

T. J. rushed into the bathroom and took her daughter's face in her hands, then folded her daughter's body into hers.

"Sinclair," she whispered. "You shouldn't have." Sinclair was too stunned to cry.

* * *

That's appalling what you made me do.
That's what my father did to me, Howard.
I'm your father?
No.

68

Who am I?

You're a man I know. A man I'm trying to figure out.

You have a real chip on your shoulder about men, don't you?

I can't imagine why.

* * *

"I fucking couldn't believe what I'd just done." He averted his eyes. He didn't want to see Dr. Glick's face. Truly, all he could see was Sinclair's shocked face after he slapped her.

"I lost complete control. I was that afraid. If something terrible had happened to her, if I'd lost her, I would kill myself." He let out a self-loathing snort. His face twitched into a humorless smile.

"What?" Glick asked.

"At least it would solve one problem. T.J. would be rid of me."

"I think she needs you, Howard."

"For what?!" His exasperation was ubiquitous and uncomprehending. A condition he lived with like a chronic disease symptom.

"Maybe she needs you to be a thorn in her side, an excuse, the husband, and the father."

He considered this.

"Well, what do you think she needs?"

"I think she needs to condescend to me, to hold me in contempt."

"Why? What does she get out of it?"

He wanted to say, "I don't fucking know, that's why I'm

here!" Instead he repeated it to himself, but he couldn't get past the sentence, the opaque words were all he could focus on. He wanted them to be a key to unlock some deep knowledge, and when Glick first uttered the question, something stirred in him that felt like a spark of insight might emerge, but it was lost in the next moment: tip of the tongue, emotional Alzheimer's. Or in therapy speak, classic resistance.

After Glick let him struggle in silence, he redirected. "And what do you need, Howard?"

"I need T.J. to love me."

The answer was immediate, emotionally bursting into painful, living technicolor. He was crying now, acting like a big baby. He covered his face with his hands, not out of embarrassment—he was well beyond that with Dr. G.—but because he felt terribly sorry for himself, and that felt righteous, and shameful, and deeply private.

He managed to say, "For two years I had what I wanted. I had T.J."

"Why do you think that stopped?"

He reached for a tissue and patted his eyes and wiped his nose.

"She smelled my need and it turned her off."

"What does that mean?"

"It means I gave away all my power and she stopped being impressed with me. She'd moved on from me, outgrown me. In some sense it was a Pygmalion thing."

"But you just said that she does need you, even if you don't like what she needs you for. Why do you think she stays? She could just divorce you."

Howard lifted his head and looked at Dr. Glick. "She needs

me," he repeated, thinking hard, slowly finding words, "because I fit into her hierarchy of needs. At bottom, at the very deepest end of the pool, in some inchoate, gender-neutral way she needs me to be this person who doesn't leave, who loves her and hates her, and to be what she secretly thinks she deserves. I am the leg in the trap that is killing you as it bleeds out and you struggle to open the jaws of death to free it because it's a part of you. It is you. I am her, she is me."

There it was. The insight.

"That's sick, isn't it?"

"No, Howard, that's human. You're human. She's human. Now the work begins."

Something frightened, but hopeful, stirred in him.

* * *

Hey, this is too intense. I need the focus off of me for a moment. I need to take a breather.

I thought you liked the attention.

I do like it, but it's also very stressful.

No problem, Howard. I love writing about T.J. She reminds me of myself.

You're hilarious, you know that? Hey, I want to ask you something. Do you look like T.J.?

No.

How old are you?

Not telling. Not important.

Wait a minute, I just had a crazy thought. I don't even know if you're a man or a woman. I just assumed you were a woman.

Why, Howard?

Are you?

What difference does it make? When I write about women I'm a woman. When I write about men I'm a man.

But in real life.

We are not here to do an author interview, Howard. You don't need answers about me. I need answers about all of you. But look, I'm doing what you asked. I'm taking the heat off you and focusing on T.J.—T.J. before you ever met her.

* * *

TEENAGE T.J.

She was screaming at her parents, shaking with rage. "I hate you!" She no longer remembered what she was so angry about, but she was sixteen, and her list of grievances was long and deep. Something had triggered the current melt down. They were in the den with the rice paper shoji screens on the windows, the plaster Buchwald sculptures, the brown tweed couch and pickled wood end tables. She felt violent. She picked up the handset on the phone sitting on the table and slammed it into the cradle over and over, screaming, "Fuck! Fuck! Fuck!"

Her mother sat tensely on the couch. Her father stood near her. She had their full attention. For once. She didn't look at them. She was gripped by her escalating rage, which felt balloon-like, untethered, and good, but it also felt utterly theatrical and done for effect. There was nowhere to go with this.

Her parents remained silent, paralyzed, when what she wanted was to be "seen" and to be stopped. Not that she would have listened to anything they had to say. But, still, they wouldn't just be staring at her like she was a rabid dog.

She strode quickly to the front door, just steps away, jerked it open and then slammed it behind her. Beneath her inflated anger was the most awful ache, a pain that she was protecting. She dug her heels into the concrete sidewalks as she moved fiercely down the neighborhood street, passing the large two and three-story houses of the newly affluent, an invented community built on sand fill, blocks from the water. She was marching to the dunes, to sit and smoke and look at the bay that opened out to the Atlantic.

She climbed straight up to the top of the first dune, her shoes uncomfortably filling with sand. She sat down and wrapped her arms around her body, clutching her pain to herself. This was an old feeling. She wished she could learn to make it stop. She wanted to go numb. But its intensity also made her feel like herself. If she would release it, it would be a kind of death.

She cupped her hands together to light a cigarette against the breeze coming off the water. She turned her body around to protect the flame and saw something out of the corner of her eye. She forgot the cigarette. She stared at her father's car, which was creeping up the street toward the dunes. As soon as she saw it, the car stopped, and her father ducked out of sight behind the steering wheel. She kept staring but the car didn't move. Had she really seen this? She waited. And in a minute her father popped back up, but when he saw her looking, he ducked down again. She turned and faced the water. She was laughing. Then she whipped back around to see the car creeping forward, jerkily stop, and her father disappear. All her rage dissipated in this comic relief. Realizing that he was afraid she'd kill herself was like he'd taken his finger and reached inside her, touching the glowing red pain in her heart. Kiss it and make it better, Daddy. And finally, she was able to cry.

* * *

Wow. I never heard this story.

Of course you haven't. I just wrote it.

You know? You said that you have sympathy for your characters, but what you just said to me had a touch of malice. You're very hard on me. I think you're the one that's angry.

Perhaps you're right. After all, I am the Author.

That's right, you have all the authority.

Yes.

***author (n.)** mid-14c., "Creator, one who brings about, one who makes or creates" someone or something, progenitor, builder, founder, trustworthy, authority, historian, responsible person, teacher, "literally" one who causes to grow.*

I'm not sure I would call you a trustworthy authority.

As compared to what, Howard? What's your frame of reference?

See what I mean? There's a nasty streak coming out here. I don't think you want to antagonize your character.

Really? What can you do to me?

I can sabotage this.

And how exactly would you do that?

Writer's block. I can quit speaking to you.

That's true, Howard. I don't want to make you upset. I love talking to you.

Fine. Just get on with the story so I can go back to bed.

You know, something is hitting a nerve here, Howard. I think I need to write a bit about you.

I don't want you to write about my family.

Why not?

It's embarrassing.

Whose family isn't?

Normal people's families aren't.

Howard, who has a normal family?

Plenty of people.

Nobody I know.

Well that speaks volumes about you, doesn't it?

Yes, and no. How many normal families do you know, Howard?

Is this a trick question?

Normalcy is something people use to feel better or worse about themselves. To me it serves no purpose. It explains nothing and is more than likely a delusion. Quick story. When I was in college I met a young woman who told me she was a debutant. I was fascinated and appalled by the world she described. Before we parted, she said, "Yes, I'm so lucky. I had a very happy childhood." If smiles could be colors I would say, she gave me a cotton candy pink smile. At the end of her freshman year, she committed suicide.

* * *

It was a cool, early spring day when Rose decided to take her four-year-old son, Howard, for a walk in the neighborhood. They had been cooped up for two days as rainstorms had passed through. Howard had fastidiously dressed himself in long khaki shorts and a green striped polo shirt. His sneakers were still white, even though he'd had them for several months. He wore his spotless, favorite blue baseball jacket. Howard had washed his face and hands and brushed his teeth before they left, all without her instructing or nagging him. Unlike his unruly, raucous older brother, Howard was an introverted child, thoughtful and sensitive. He was also beautiful. Women would stop and talk to him on the street and in the supermarket, exclaiming, "Who's the pretty baby?!", "What a handsome boy you are!" He had long black eyelashes that framed his shining blue eyes. His lustrous, thick brown hair and fine features gave him a feminine beauty that deeply disturbed Rose. He didn't act like normal little boys or look like them. His intelligence frightened her. It made her feel inadequate, like she wasn't up to the job of being the parent to the child. Just this year he had taught himself to read. She didn't want a gifted child. She wanted a boy like everyone else's boy. She felt intimidated. He asked her questions she couldn't answer. "Are stars small holes in the sky where light shines from behind? What's the behind? Why do grownups have hair on their legs and arms? Can I have a monkey?" Other little boys wanted dogs. He wanted a monkey.

So on this lovely, sun-lit morning, full of puddles and rivulets of water rushing to sewer drains, they walked to Prospect Park. She watched Howard avoid stepping into anything that would soil his sneakers. He walked on his tiptoes when that was a possibility. Once in the park he avoided walking on the grass and stuck to the pavement. He walked a few feet ahead of her, lost in his own thoughts. Something about his carefulness, his fear of getting dirty, her fear of his growing up to be a "faygela" made her speed up behind him and push him into a large mud puddle. He went in face first and she rushed to lift him up, dripping and covered in mud. He was screaming as she held him. She kissed his tear-streaked face, "Shhhh, shhhh. It's okay, Howard, it's only dirt."

* * *

Yes, my mother told me this story, but she told it funny. She told it to amuse people about me as a child. The way you tell it is heartbreaking.

That's because it wasn't a funny story.

You know, you just changed P.O.V. You wrote this from Rose's perspective. You can't do that. She's not a character in the book. You also gave me agency. You gave me a memory that was different from the one you wrote. You can't do that. Aren't there rules about this?

Yes. Maybe my editor will make me change it.

You have an editor?

Not yet.

You're pretty optimistic.

I am.

What's so special about this book?

I can't explain it. Read the book.

Very funny. You must crack yourself up.

I do sometimes.

I want a happy ending.

I don't know what the ending is yet, Howard.

No, but if you care anything about me, you'll give me one.

I want good things for you, Howard. I really do.

Then give them to me.

In time. It will happen in time. But right this minute, what I'm writing about you is extremely sad.

* * *

"Why aren't you wearing the new shirt I bought you, Howard?"

Howard didn't answer and continued watching the T.V.

"Howard, I'm talking to you...Howard!"

"What?"

"I asked you a question. Look at me."

His mother had moved in front of the T.V., blocking his view. He looked up at her. She was one of the most beautiful women he'd ever seen. Movie star beautiful. He couldn't understand how his father had ever attracted her—a high school math teacher with thinning hair who was always sucking on breath mints and clearing his throat. He didn't get it. He didn't like his father much. But then again, his father didn't like him much.

When he was a teenager, he once asked Rose, "Why did you marry him?"

"Everyone else went off to the war," she said. "Not him. I thought, now this is a smart man."

She'd paused, hand on hip, her cigarette perched between two fingers. She'd narrowed her eyes as the smoke rose.

"He had hair in those days."

He laughed, because she laughed. It was a nice moment of mother and son sharing contempt for the same man.

It wasn't until he was a grown up and she was old that he found out that she'd been engaged to an incredibly handsome fighter pilot who'd been killed in the war. His father, Lou, was his best friend. After the funeral, he'd made a beeline for Rose.

"I never got over it," she said. For a fleeting moment her face became anguished. He wanted to look away in embarrassment as though he'd just seen his mother naked. He was not used to seeing her as human.

Then she dropped the other shoe.

"He cheated on me."

Mr. Magoo, his father, Lou?! had cheated on this smart, beautiful, (albeit depressed, insecure, critical) woman?

"Why not?" she said. "Men can do anything they want."

The long ash from her cigarette fell off before making it to the ashtray, soiling the front of her blouse. Something the ever-elegant Rose would never have let happen in her younger years. "Being old is a constant indignity," she said, brushing the ash from her blouse and further succeeding in soiling herself.

His mother didn't die from lung cancer as he'd expected. She died of heart complications. They called it heart failure.

* * *

Reads like a punch line.

Do you have any sympathy, Howard? You are so cut off.

You're avoiding what I said.

80

Yes, okay. I'm afraid of that too. It's hard to know what works when you're writing. It's all just throwing coins into a wishing well.

* * *

"Look at me when you speak to me, Howard."

"I can't wear the shirt."

He felt his eyes watering, not because he felt like crying, but because looking at his mother was like staring into the sun. He lowered his eyes to the beige carpeted floor, a color he absolutely hated. It was the color mucous would be if you mixed it with poop.

"Why can't you?"

"Because it will make my old shirts sad." He looked up, hoping she'd understand.

Not a chance. She was staring at him like she did when she thought he was being abnormal.

"What are you talking about, Howard?"

"My other shirts will feel like I don't like them anymore."

She reached into the pocket of her skirt and took out a pack of cigarettes, tapped one out and stuck it in her mouth. She took out her lighter from the other pocket and flicked it, lighting the cigarette tip. She inhaled deeply, blew the smoke out, and contemplated her son. Then she moved out of the way of the T.V. and left the room.

* * *

Does this woman ever not smoke? That's the only descrip-

tion you've given her. You said she was beautiful. What did she look like?

That's what you want to know?

Did you just sigh at me?

Yes.

But before you tell me what she looked like, I just want to tell you something.

Yes?

I completely get how I felt about the shirts. How old was I? Six? Seven?

You were nine, Howard.

Well, I still have sympathy for inanimate objects. Mostly ones with faces. When Sinclair was little, and we'd go to a toy store, as we walked past the dolls or the stuffed animals, I would start speaking in a falsetto voice.

"Please don't leave me here! Give this teddy a home!"

"Rosie, who said that?"

Sinclair would shrug her shoulders and giggle.

"It's me, the brown bear with the red heart."

They were all brown bears with red hearts.

"You have to find him, Rosie!"

As Sinclair looked and looked, getting closer to one of the many teddies on the shelf, I'd say, "You're getting warmer... Warmer... You're hot!" until she was standing directly in front of one bear. "Yes! Yes! It's me!" And she would pick up the bear and hug it to herself while I beamed at them both, trying not to burst into tears.

Howard.

It's okay. It's okay. I'll tell you a funny story. T.J. and I had gone on vacation to Maine back in the good old days, and we *went crazy eating lobster plucked fresh from the sea. We had lobster everyday we were there. About six months after we'd gotten back, we had a terrible lobster craving, so we went to a seafood place in the neighborhood. As we approached the lobster tank to pick one out, I said, "Help! Help!" Seeing those live, sluggish, lobsters crowded and stressed in that tank, just so that I could eat one, made me feel sick. "Help! Please don't eat me!"*

I looked at T.J. "I can't."

We turned around and walked out of the restaurant. I haven't eaten lobster since.

I love you, Howard.

You mean, LOVE, love?

No. I mean I love who you are.

Isn't that a bit narcissistic since you've already told me that I'm you?

Well, that just broke the mood. Don't be so literal about you being me.

But tell the truth. Isn't this how you feel about dollies and stuffed animals?

Yes. But it turns out there are lots of people that feel this way.

People you know?

Well, Facebook friends.

Virtual friends. Do you have many make-believe playmates?

You, Howard. You, and T.J., and Rose, and Sinclair. You're all my imaginary playmates.

Do you ever leave the house? I'm just asking.

No more chit chat. What was it we were talking about again?

Jesus. You already know.

Oh right. Yes, what did Rose look like? She looked a lot like you, Howard. You have her thick, naturally wavy, dark brown hair—or had, until you turned salt and pepper—and you have her eyelashes. Your whole life women have envied your eyelashes. Not fair that they should be on a man. But your mother's eyes were violet, not blue.

Nice combination, dark brown and violet.

Yes, striking.

Unlike the women you usually go for, she was very curvy, had a body built for male creature comfort: wide hips, full chest, and a narrow waist. And long legs. Kind of a classic body; a body that never goes out of style, despite changes in fashion—corsets, stretched necks, broken feet, bound chests, bullet bras, girdles. When the clothes come off it's a body that gets reached for, admired, desired by men the world over.

Men desire all bodies, all types, of all women, all over the world.

Yes, but hers was a classic, all the right baby-making cues. The biologically favored model.

I remember her ankles and her shoes.

* * *

Howard was lying on the carpeted living room floor under the piano watching his mother's red high-heeled shoes work the pedals of their baby grand piano. Rose gave piano lessons and sometimes, after a student left, she'd play and sing. When he was still a boy, he'd lie there and listen. She should have been a professional, she was that good. Howard wished he could sing, but he had no voice. His mother would remind him of this whenever he unconsciously broke into song. "Howard. Please." She had perfect pitch and it was painful for her to hear him go flat.

Sometimes he fell asleep on the carpet, lulled by the sonorous humming and breathing of the wood, her dulcet alto rising while she caressed the keys.

You do realize how sexual this sounds.

Of course.

This was the most intimate they were together. She was not a toucher. She must have held him as a baby, but truly he had no memory of being hugged. She must have physically cared for him when he was sick, but after the age of five, it was thermometers in the mouth, and pills to swallow, and goodnight. He would sometimes catch her looking at him. In an unguarded moment he thought he could see love. But she would turn away, and become occupied with whatever chore needed her attention.

Well, he was a chore that needed her attention.

His older bother, Merv, was his father's son. When they were little kids, Merv followed his father around, fawning. His father liked to give his boys verbal math problems to solve. Howard could do these in his sleep, but he didn't want to give his father the satisfaction of making him compete with his moron brother. He would pretend to listen to the tricky problem, but then his brain would shut down. He didn't even try to think about it. Merv always got the correct answer, rewarded by a hearty "That's right!" from his father. Howard would pretend to be absorbed in the complicated picture puzzle he was working on, or the book he was reading. To tune them out he would invent another version to amuse himself. Something completely dumb. In his story, someone always died.

Problem: One man gets on a train in Syracuse, NY at 2:00 in the afternoon. His wife had made him a lunch of three hardboiled eggs. Another man gets on the train at 2:30 p.m. His wife had made him a ham sandwich. The train is traveling at 60 m.p.h. Another train, that left the station traveling in the opposite direction, was also traveling at 60 miles per hour. What color was the jacket of the man with the ham sandwich?

Answer: The first man choked on a hardboiled egg because his wife hadn't packed him anything to drink. The second man got off the train because he had left his blue jacket in the train station and it had a check for ten thousand dollars in the pocket. He left his paper bag with his sandwich behind on his seat. A shabbily dressed man got on at another stop and sat down next to the ham sandwich, which he promptly ate. Within seconds he started to gag, his eyes bulged out of their sockets and foam dribbled from his mouth. And then he collapsed. Dead. Poisoned. The other passenger didn't see any of this because he was also dead, sitting with his mouth open, hardboiled egg spilling from his tongue and lips and down the front of his shirt.

Howard would laugh and his father would glare. "What's so funny?"

Merv would spring on him and get him in a headlock, giving him noogies with his knuckles as hard as he could into his scalp. This also made his father laugh.

Rose sent him to a neighborhood public school even though he had an I.Q. of 160. His father approved of the choice, considering the fact that he taught in a public school.

They didn't want their son to grow up feeling he was superior to other kids. She wanted him to be regular.

He was beaten up every day.

He toughened up. He became an asshole, a bully. Just like a real boy. This still didn't make her happy. It made her feel guilty, so she distanced herself even further. Plus, he'd managed to embarrass her in a new way. She was always being called up to school to meet with the principal, or one of his teachers. But how much could they complain, really? He got straight A's. School was so easy. He didn't have to work at all.

He discovered a new power in high school. He was great with the ladies. He stopped fighting and started fucking. He bought his girlfriends perfume right before he broke up with them, the same scent his mother always wore. He didn't stay in a relationship for long. He didn't have to. He was in demand.

And then, he found the drums. All the other instruments had been assigned in music class and only the drums were left. And he fell in love. Something he could beat the shit out of, something he could practice at home and drive his family crazy with—and they couldn't object. He was getting credit for it in school. He was in band.

"Why can't you play guitar like the other boys?" Rose would ask, and he would grin. Revenge is a dish best served cold.

* * *

Ya wanna know what I think?
Yes, of course, Howard.

I think you're being glib about how you describe my childhood.

It's hard. It's hard to write about this. Actually, it depresses me. Because I know Rose actually felt guilty and torn. She did love you Howard, but her coldness, her distance really wasn't about you. It was about herself. But understanding isn't the same thing as repair.

And me? What was I feeling? What did I think?

You felt the worst thing a child can feel, fundamentally undeserving of love. You did what any good survivor does. You compartmentalized and lost access to parts of yourself that you then spend the rest of your life trying to recover.

Oh, God.

I'm sorry, Howard.

But I'm a good parent. I was there for Sinclair. I was both a mother and father to her.

Yes, you were, Howard, but she also had a real mother. T.J.

* * *

Sinclair started sleepwalking when she was seven. T.J. was traveling a lot and when she came home she and Howard bickered and fought. Because T.J. was gone so much Howard pretty much slept in the same bed with Sinclair to comfort her. T.J. protested about this. She thought it was unhealthy, but who was she to say anything?

One night, after T.J. had been gone for two weeks, then came home, Sinclair had been made to sleep in her own bed. Howard tiptoed out once she'd gone under while he was reading to her.

Lying in their bed, Howard snoring beside her, T.J. was too wound up to sleep. As she lay there with her eyes open, curled up on her side, her back to Howard, she saw this apparition coming toward her.

"Sinclair," she whispered.

No answer. Sinclair just kept coming closer. And then she got into the bed, not on Howard's side, but in bed next to her. She threw her arms around T.J.'s body and wrapped her legs around her legs and held on tight. T.J. was afraid to move. Sinclair clung to her like a starfish. If T.J. moved at all she moved with her, reasserting her hold, eliminating any space between them.

T.J. stayed awake all night. She stayed on her side in that one position 'til morning. She felt like weeping tears of blood.

When Howard woke up in the very early morning and saw T.J. and Sinclair together, he quietly slipped out of bed, gently pulled Sinclair off T.J. and carried her back to her own bed.

Sinclair had no memory of this ever happening. T. J. never forgot it. The next day she left again.

* * *

I wish you hadn't written this. I wish I didn't know about it.

I wish it had never happened.

I'm not going to ask.

Don't ask.

I should never have named Sinclair, Rose, or called her Rosie. It was like giving her a curse.

No, Howard, you were trying to break the curse.

My mother, Sinclair, you. What is it with women? All men want is your tenderness, your love. Why is that so hard?

That's what women want, too, Howard. What we all want. I'm interested in the reasons we feel deprived.

So, go on. Tell me about T.J.

* * *

T.J.'s father, the architect, disdained anything that wasn't ultra-modern. He designed the house they lived in with soaring ceilings and huge, uncovered windows, rectangular rooms, and clean white walls. No recesses or nooks, no L-shaped spaces that disappeared from view around corners. The bedrooms and bathrooms, of course, had doors, and there was a door to his study, which was sequestered at the very top of the house, reachable by its own set of stairs. His room was an exception to his own rules of grandeur. It was low ceilinged with no windows, and had cherry wood paneling that, when pressed in just the right places, opened up onto hidden shelves containing all his books and papers. Here, he was allowed his secrets, his privacy. The only furnishings were a twin bed, a glass and chrome desk, black leather chair, and a stainless steel lamp. To look at the room, you would have thought, "What you see is what you get."

Once upon a time, in a land far, far away, when her daddy was king, and she was his princess, it had been her favorite room in the house.

It was also a house designed to silence. All the floors were covered in the same plush, royal blue carpet that coursed, like a river, over the stairs from the very top of the house, down to the very bottom, hushing the patter of feet, deadening sound.

T.J. brought the noise.

T.J. was more or less an accident. Her mother and father had given up on trying, and then, when they weren't looking, while Sarah was reading a magazine and Ross was polishing his car, *voilà*, pregnant. It came as such a shock, and by then, they were so used to their life as a couple, it was hard to see how a child would fit in. Reconciling themselves, they began to make space for their son. It had to be a boy. Whatever would they do with a girl? Girls made emotional demands. Sarah wasn't sure she could cope. Ross wanted a boy to eventually run his firm: Ross Parker and Son.

When squalling, black-haired T.J. arrived, the name Thomas James Parker was converted to T.J. Parker. They bought new baby clothes, but the blue wallpaper with its climbing vines of dark blue leaves remained. There wouldn't be a "pink for girls" theme in baby T.J.'s world. It was blues and greens and yellows. T.J.'s favorite color was red. When she became a teenager, she insisted they strip the walls of her room and paint it China red. She furnished it with antiques that she found at thrift stores, such as an oak roll-topped desk, a Victorian hurricane lamp, a red and white striped silk chaise lounge. Her mother got her anything she wanted, just to keep her quiet. Her daughter often pressed on her very last nerve.

T.J.'s mother, Sarah, was a descendent from one of the obscure but still blood-related line of Eastman's. She was tall and willowy. She gleamed like she'd been polished. And she had. Finishing schools. Vassar. A small stint as a model and then whisked off her feet, literally, by Ross—a man who could dance.

"May I?" he'd asked, having walked across the enormous dance floor to bow and extend his hand. As soon as she was in his arms, she realized that she had never really had a dance partner before. No matter how inexpertly she moved, she couldn't make a mistake; she was protectively cupped in the palms of his hands. She relaxed into him, allowing his six-foot-three body to command her five-foot, eleven-and-a-half inches. It was effortless, and he made her feel graceful, not something the tallest girl everywhere typically felt.

She arched her back away from him, his arm securing her waist, and looked into his eyes. "If you're not already married, will you marry me?"

He looked at her quite seriously and said nothing. He didn't have to. She knew.

Sarah became an interior decorator after they married. She loved Japanese art, clean lines, and serenity. If Ross was in charge of designing their house, Sarah was the one who decorated it. Each choice she made was a gift to him. He was barred from a room until she was done and then, hands cupped over his eyes, she would lead him in and then expectantly await his approval. All she needed was his smile that would slowly spread over his face as he took in her ideas and her arrangements.

In the den downstairs, their family room, she installed sliding, rice paper shoji screens on the windows that filtered the light and created a soft, lambent whiteness at one end of the room. Along another entire wall she had a fish tank built in that was twenty feet long and eight feet high. She stocked it with tropical fish, sea horses, snails and starfish, and created

an undersea world of coral, rocks, shells, plants, and minia-
ture castles. The blue-green light, the patterns of swimming
fish, and the underwater feel of the room created a place of
calm and meditation. As a child, T.J. would spend hours
watching, and talking to the fish, making up stories in her
head about her actually living in the tank with them and the
secret life she shared with her fish family.

* * *

You know, I never knew T.J.'s parents.

Why is that, Howard?

*Let's see, I'm thirteen years older than her, a musician, a
writer, and a Jew. I think it was the Jew part that was the last
straw.*

Did she ever say why they were so estranged?

Nope.

Did they ever see Sinclair?

Nope.

Can you stop saying "Nope?"

Make me.

You're funny.

Maybe they died in a skiing accident in an avalanche.

Really? Whose book do you think you're in?

*Point taken. Okay, get on with it. I'm steeling myself for
the revelations. The suspense is killing me.*

We can do without the sarcasm.

Is this the royal "we"?

Shut up, Howard.

You must be onto something really upsetting, because

you're getting very testy.

* * *

When T.J. was very young when she had recurring dreams about her mother trying to kill her. There were several versions. One was that she and her mother were walking home after dark. A mammoth hole in the ground stood between them and their house. Only a small strip of dirt edged this abyss.

"Go on, T.J. Keep walking."

There was enough room to go single file and her mother hung back while she hesitantly walked ahead.

"Don't stop, T.J. Go!"

She very carefully put one foot in front of the other, her hand touching the side of the house for balance, but there was nothing to hold onto. A clod of earth broke away and she tumbled into the hole that had no bottom. As she fell, rolling over and over, she became a ball that grew smaller. As she plummeted she felt herself disappearing.

It was her daddy who came into her room to comfort her. "It's okay, baby."

She threw her arms around him, wailing, and he lifted her onto his lap, wiping his big hands over her sweating brow, pushing her damp hair from her face. Then he cupped her head in his hand and pulled her into his chest and into his arms, surrounding her with safety. "It was only a dream," he would repeat soothingly, kissing the top of her head. "Shhhh, shhhh."

Her dreams formed two of her basic beliefs: that being

alive came without a safety net, and that death was complete erasure.

In real life, when she and her mother went for walks on the city streets, T.J. would always nervously watch her mother and, if she wandered too close to the curb and the traffic, T.J. would say, "Be carefy, Mommy. Be carefy." She was afraid that her mother would wander into the cars and be instantly killed. She worried about her mother's survival; it was a constant anxiety. As was her fear about her mother's withdrawal when she was angry with her. It made her desperate to get back into her good graces.

When she was little, she would climb onto something to make herself tall enough to get her arms around her mother's neck and look into her eyes. "Please, Mommy, let's be friends again." It usually worked. Her mother would sigh, or smile, and nod her head, and sometimes, her mother would put her arms around her and hug her close.

"Mommy, I'm tired," she whined.

Sarah was carrying a bag of groceries and her pocket book, and holding onto T.J.'s hand.

T.J. had stopped in the middle of the sidewalk and was making that snuffling, weepy sound that irritated Sarah so much. She gave T.J.'s hand a yank to get her moving.

"We're almost home, T.J."

The tug worked, but she dragged the tip of one shoe behind her, took a step, and then dragged the other one.

This is where the story became impossible. It couldn't have happened.

Sarah dropped her hand and walked over to the curb

where a truck was parked. The driver was standing on the sidewalk, smoking a cigarette. Sarah pointed to T.J. while smiling at the driver. As T.J. walked up to her mother, she heard, "Could you please drive my daughter home?"

T.J. said nothing. Her whimpering stopped. She was petrified into silence.

The stranger lifted her onto the front seat of the truck cab. High above the ground, everything looked far away. She felt so little, like a small package of a blue dress with white ankle socks and red shoes, left on a seat, to be delivered.

She couldn't remember anything beyond the truck pulling away and feeling helpless, and looking back at her mother who was waving—going, going—all gone.

* * *

No mother does this.

I don't know.

But it can't be real.

As real as memory.

What is memory?

Who we are.

I have memories.

I know.

Then am I real?

You are becoming more and more real as the story continues, don't you agree?

But what was I before the story began?

What was the world before the Big Bang?

I can never get a satisfying answer from you.

Because, the truth is, Howard, I don't know.

* * *

From the ages of two to four, her dreams and reality were often confused. Her memories were so old and worn from being recalled over a lifetime that she no longer knew for certain how much she invented or embellished every time she looked back. She only knew that the feeling of what was real was distinct and vivid from her dream memories. Neither corresponded to the possible, though both were accurate to her life.

Her scariest dream was very banal. She would wake up in the dark. It was hard to see, so she flipped the light switch, but the light didn't come on. As her eyes grew accustomed to the dark, she saw that the room looked exactly like her room, but was the negative version of it. Her father had shown her the negatives that pictures developed from. She loved looking at the ghosted images, holding them up to the light, trying to recognize people and places in their black and white worlds. She realized in her nightmare, that she was trapped in a negative, and that she didn't have the power to make it go positive, to develop into normal.

* * *

God. Was there anything happy in T.J.'s childhood?
I'm sure there was.
Well, why aren't you writing about that?
Because, I'm trying to show what you and T.J. have in common.

Cold mothers?

Ambivalent mothers.

Your mother must have been a doozy.

This isn't about my mother.

You know what? This book isn't about me. It's about you. You were one fucked up little girl.

* * *

Howard was visiting friends in the country. He was sitting on a chair beneath a plated glass window that looked out onto the porch. He was mid-sentence in a conversation about his dreams, when he felt something hit the top of his head and break over him.

"Don't move!" his friend Alice screamed.

He was stunned and didn't know what was happening. A trickle of something red and wet dripped into his eye.

"Don't move!" Alice screamed again.

Her husband, Paul, was standing over him, picking large shards of glass off of him. He was told that he was wearing a necklace of broken glass. At the ER they said how lucky he was to be alive, another millimeter and it would have severed his carotid artery. For days after, he had the surreal experience of feeling like he was living on borrowed time.

* * *

Am I living on borrowed time? I guess you couldn't kill me off. You just wanted to scare the shit out of me. I get the message. I'll shut up about it. You could still change your mind and kill me off before the end of the book, you know, completely surprising your readers.

I wouldn't do that, Howard. The book is called Helping Howard.

Maybe its meaning is metaphysical. I could still die. Maybe helping me is to put me out of my misery.

You know? I hadn't considered that.

I was joking. Death is not the answer.

You're right. You're right. Can I get on with the story?

It's the backstory. Are we ever going to return to the present?

Of course we are, but right now we're living in the past.

You know that's not where I live. I live in the future. I always have. The future you concoct for me, one piece of the past at a time.

So you don't subscribe to living in the present?

There's no such thing. Technically speaking, it takes eighty milliseconds before the brain puts together all the data being perceived and constructs a conscious "you." So, in fact, we're always experiencing the past. And the moment we're in now, what we call the present is actually the unknown future because the brain hasn't comprehended it yet.

You must read the same books I do.

Ha ha. But hey, I appreciate your attributing some of the smart things to me. You could hog them all to yourself.

Has it ever occurred to you, Howard, that the Author is just another character? That someone else is writing this book?

Nooo. That makes my head want to explode. And you've terrified me... Wait, you're just fucking with me. It's not fair because I can't see you smile.

Okay, I'll nod my head.

You are sadistic.

I just think I'm funny.

I don't know who you are.

That's because I move in mysterious ways.

You have a God complex. I'm in the hands of an insane person.

I'm ignoring you, Howard.

Yes, that would be consistent with being God.

I have other lives to deal with. It's not just about you.

SARAH

The day she married Ross their life together became her most precious adornment, her dearest possession. Women remarked, "How well marriage suits you." Men murmured, "You've never looked lovelier."

Before T.J. was born, when Ross came home from work he would always seek her out and give her a hug and kiss. Sometimes he'd waltz her around and sing in her ear and dinner would be later than usual. He brought her fresh flowers. She put notes in his pockets. She awakened to "Hi, beautiful." But now when Ross came home, T.J. shouted, "Daddy's home!" and ran to him, throwing her arms around his legs, and it was T.J. who got scooped up and kissed on the cheek.

While taking a roast out of the oven, or setting the table, or pouring herself another glass of chardonnay, she'd think, *he* gets to waltz in and be adored, while *she* gets the poopy diapers, the tantrums, and coaxing food into their daughter, and entertaining her, and, and, and...

They had agreed that until T.J. was school-aged, Sarah would stay home and be the full-time mom. They hardly ever went out, saw friends, or entertained anymore. She was too exhausted and T.J. never wanted to go to sleep. It was a pitched battle every night.

And Ross was working longer hours and spending less time at home, certainly much less time with her. When he was home, T.J. monopolized him.

He spoke to T.J. like she was a favorite pet. "Who's my pretty girl? Who's my smart girl? Who's the big girl?" He stroked the top of her head while she played at his feet. He put her on his lap and showed her books of photos of famous buildings from around the world, sometimes of places he'd designed.

When T.J. needed something, it was, "Mommy, Mommy, Mommy!"

But when she was her most delightful, affectionate self, it was only, "Daddy."

Sarah didn't talk about it to anyone. She couldn't talk about it to Ross. He fended her off, annoyed and disappointed that she couldn't handle the job of being a mother. "One child, Sarah. T.J. is your only job."

She couldn't confide in her friends. Everyone thought she had the perfect life and marriage. She didn't want anyone feeling sorry for her. And would they? Complaining about her life felt like a privileged whine. It was embarrassing.

No, there was something wrong with her. She would never have known it if she hadn't had a child. Maybe she would have felt differently if she'd had a son. Ross would have still been hers.

No, she didn't like this one bit. She wanted everything back the way it was.

"Mommy!" T.J. would shriek as soon as she lay down, because T.J. got bored easily and never napped. Sarah was *it*. The uneasy detente between mother and child was fragile. Both of them were often on the verge of screaming. This was something new for Sarah. She'd become a screamer and a hitter: a punisher. Ross didn't know. Ross wasn't home enough to know.

Guilty as charged, Your Honor. Guilty of having no patience, guilty of doing everything wrong, guilty of feeling guilty instead of changing, guilty of being a bad mother.

T.J. was her first failure. Ross hated a loser.

* * *

She sounds like a monster.

But she isn't a monster, although, she thinks she is.

She shouldn't have had children.

You're probably right. There are plenty of women who shouldn't have had children.

Do you have children?

No.

Ever wanted them?

No.

Why?

Maybe, because I remember what it was like to be a child, or I fear the future of this planet, or I couldn't risk fucking up another human being. Besides, there are too many people in the world already.

Sounds like good reasons, but I don't buy them. I think you were just scared.

Okay, yes, the thought of having a child terrified me.

T.J.

When she was little she couldn't wait until her daddy got home. He was the sunshine that came into the house. Even her mother smiled and got happy. But when her daddy would hug her mommy she would be so jealous that she would wedge herself between them.

"Daddy, don't hurt my mommy!" She wanted her daddy to hug her, but it was her mommy's legs that she wrapped herself around protectively. It was so confusing. Her daddy and mommy laughed and separated and Daddy would pat her head and leave the kitchen, or lift her up and carry her to the den with him. She looked back over her shoulder and saw the sadness in her mommy's eyes. She always knew what her mommy was feeling because she felt it, too. Even when she was getting a spanking and hated her, she also knew that her mommy was not just angry but was also feeling sorry. She said, "I'm sorry" a lot to T.J. Her mommy was tired all the time. T.J. knew that she "wore her out." But she couldn't not. She couldn't stop being T.J. She wouldn't know how. Just like her mommy couldn't stop being Mommy. Nobody knew how to be different.

Her daddy didn't have to change because he was perfect.

And then, he wasn't.

About when she turned six, she started to notice that her daddy was not so nice to her mommy. She started to notice and feel all the bad feelings. Why didn't he see them, too? Didn't he care?

The sadder her mommy got, the more her daddy's ebullience and good cheer became less like sunshine and more like the best vacation place she couldn't visit anymore. She didn't like her mommy. She loved her daddy so much. On the other hand, she felt so guilty and sad about how unhappy her mommy was that she just had to take her side. Daddy became the stranger in the family. He didn't know that he was being kicked out. He seemed to not know anything, ever. He didn't know he was losing T.J. She was angry about that. Her mother was her survival. Her daddy was her playmate and protector. But her daddy was never home.

* * *

It's amazing that the woman I've slept next to all these years has never told me any of this.

Have you ever asked?

Of course I have. But she's always refused to talk about her family.

106

What did you tell Sinclair?

The truth. That T.J. doesn't talk to her parents or see them.

And Sinclair doesn't ask why?

Sure she does. Or did. T.J. would start frowning, or rubbing her neck to ease the tension. And if that didn't work and Sinclair persisted, she'd get hostile. "Why are you asking? What do you care? It has nothing to do with you."

"Other people have grandparents," Sinclair would complain. "Or aunts and uncles. Cousins. Even brothers and sisters."

"Well you have a mother and father. I'm afraid that's all you get. Some children don't even have that. You have a roof over your head and get three meals a day. I'd say you're a lucky kid."

"But what do I tell people?"

"Tell 'people' it's none of their goddamn business."

Speaking of Sinclair, can we get back to my daughter?

What do you want to know about her?

Is she safe?

Of course not. She's a teenager.

* * *

Sinclair didn't tell her parents the truth about why she was out all night. She said that she fell asleep on the train coming home from her friend's house. When she woke up she was at the end of the line somewhere way the hell out in Brooklyn. She was disoriented and made the wrong connections getting back and more time was wasted. She did own up to staying too late and breaking her promise about when she'd be home. That made being lost on the trains all night credible. What time did she leave? 3:00 a.m.

"3:00 A.M.?!"

Grounded.

"If we still lived in the city, this wouldn't have happened," she said. That was good. Get them on the defensive.

Howard glowered at T.J.

T.J. said, "You're an idiot," and got up from the kitchen table and left the room. Since T.J. didn't look at either of them when she said it, neither of them knew which one of them she meant it for, so both of them took it personally.

There was definitely tension in the house for a few days, but then T.J. announced she had rented a house on Fire Island from a friend, for a three-day weekend.

They'd never been on Fire Island in October before. They had been going there since Sinclair was a kid to escape the oppressive summer heat in the city. T.J. was a swimmer. Every morning she would get up early and swim for an hour. Not Sinclair. When she was little, the ocean frightened her. She preferred getting her feet wet, or building sand castles with Howard, until she outgrew that. Why do you outgrow such things?

She loved the damp and salt in everything. Their cottage rentals were soggy and pungent, but all the smells were good since they were associated with times all three of them were together. Howard and T.J. would even do unusual things like walk together holding hands, and after some wine, they might even kiss in front of her.

Walking on the crisscross of the boardwalk planks all over

the island was magical—no cars, no shoes, no rules. Everyone relaxed.

She had the photos to prove it. Her handsome parents smiling for the camera, arms around each other. Her father holding her in his arms, lifting her hand to wave at the camera with a big grin on her face. The picture of her mother in her one-piece bathing suit, her legs in the surf, leaning back on her flattened palms, fingers splayed in the sand, laughing. They were happy. They were smiling. The photo albums don't lie, do they?

Then T.J. announced that she had invited her girlfriend, Cherie, to go with them.

Sinclair liked Cherie. She was a petite, merry red-head who laughed a lot and was smart and loud and often made Sinclair laugh when she made fun of T.J. This originally shocked Sinclair. No one ever made fun of T.J. But Cherie also made fun of Howard, and he hated her for that.

Sinclair carried folding beach chairs, while Cherie pulled the two bags of groceries in one of the wagons that were ubiquitous on the Island. Also, piled into the wagon were their canvas bags with their essentials.

One of the most noticeable things about the Island, off-season, was that all the people were gone. Houses were boarded up. The day-trippers and summer tourists pretty much disappeared after Labor Day. To the small, hard-core population of year-rounders, this was probably the best time of the year. But to Sinclair, the island looked sadly abandoned. They were alone.

They trudged, single file, on the boardwalk up to the house and dumped everything inside. The house had that delicious mildewed smell of her memories, which would change once they lit the logs in the fireplace.

Long gone were the naïve days of her youth when she believed her parents had a conventional marriage. She knew her mother was gay. But T.J. wasn't openly gay around Sinclair until she turned twelve. She continued to believe her parents loved each other and simultaneously believed they were profoundly ill matched. She couldn't think about the question that plagued her: why were they together? She was fiercely protective of Howard, but she also held him in contempt. When she started to see him through T.J.'s eyes she began the descent into losing respect for him, which was terribly hard on her, because she loved him. She was the chewed gum on the bottom of their shoes that stretched elastically when they lifted their feet, forcing them back to terra firma. It was her job to keep them together, and so, she never told them the truth about her own life. She had to be happy, normal, not give them any problems. Nobody knew how Sinclair felt, or what she needed. Disconnection seemed to be the preferred survival tool in her family. And she did disconnect.

During one of T.J. and Howard's particularly egregious arguments, their rancid words entering her bedroom like bad gas, she couldn't take it anymore and she called her best friend, Marci. They went dancing. They both had fake I.D.s, and really, if you were good looking and you sucked up to the gatekeeper at the head of the line, you could get in to just about any club.

They got stoned and danced their asses off. At one point, Sinclair twisted her ankle, but kept on going.

Marci was the leader. She could get Sinclair into trouble in a heartbeat. They were sitting at a two-top taking a break, all sweaty and flushed. Marci flagged down the waiter passing by and said to Sinclair, "Watch this."

She shouted instructions over the din of the club. She pointed to two guys at the bar.

When the waiter left, Sinclair leaned in and asked, "What did you say?"

"I just bought both those guys drinks, on us."

"You what?"

"I've always wanted to do that. Dudes in rom coms are always doing that kind of shit."

"I don't want them to come over here."

"Shhh. Just watch."

Sinclair saw the waiter delivering Marci's message and pointing to them. The guys looked surprised and pleased. Delighted, actually. They raised their glasses and nodded. Thanks.

Marci raised her glass and nodded back.

In a moment, the two dudes were standing beside their table.

"Ladies, may we join you?"

They were both wearing suits. Who wears suits to a club? They were straight looking. Clean cut. Businessmen. This was them loosening up and slumming, she supposed. Guys on the make, bright young stars on the rise at their firms. Both were in the financial sector. That's what they said, "The financial sector."

She made up nicknames for them, Manson and the Unibomber, Tweedledee and Tweedledumber, while Marci flirted so overtly that Sinclair was deeply embarrassed for her. Marci was nodding her head in Sinclair's direction and saying something about her. Brown Hair—one had brown hair and one had blonde hair—was smiling at her. Blondie couldn't be bothered; he only had eyes for Marci.

"Wanna dance?"

She looked over at Marci, who was leaning into Blondie and saying something. She shrugged and stood up, vaguely aware that her ankle inside her boot throbbed.

They danced. Neither of them connected. He made some overtures by moving into her space, trying to get his pelvis to make contact, but she danced away. Facing each other, he bent forward and yelled, "What's with the short hair?"

She touched her head and said, "You like it?"

"Not really," he yelled back. "I like long hair on girls."

"I'm not a girl."

"What?"

She wasn't sure he heard her.

"I'm a woman."

His eyes roved over her body. Grinning, he said, "Yup, you're definitely a woman."

He was such a schmuck.

"What's with the suit?" she yelled.

"I came right from work."

"Undertaker?"

"What?"

"You're an undertaker?"

"Financial Analyst," forgetting that he'd already told her during the introductions.

Not just straight, but stupid, too. No sense of humor.

The song stopped and Sinclair went to sit down.

Marci was paying their bill.

"What are you doing?"

"Don't sit down. Come on. We're leaving."

"Where to?"

"We're going to Ric's place. He has a penthouse near the United Nations. I want to see it."

"Are you kidding me?"

Marci grabbed her by the elbow and pulled her aside. "Look, it's an adventure. It'll be interesting. Come on, it'll be fun. Something we'll laugh about when we're thirty, or married with children."

Sinclair felt trapped, like she had no free will.

"I don't want to be alone. You've got to come."

In the elevator, just before the top floor, Marci pressed the stop button. As if Sinclair and Brown Hair weren't there, Marci pushed Blondie back against the wall and started kissing him.

While her best friend made out with a representative of the Aryan race, she and Brown Hair stood about awkwardly. The moment didn't last very long because Blondie lifted Marci up and she wrapped her legs around him. He freed one hand to punch the elevator button. They were moving again. Stopping at the 18th floor, the elevator doors opened onto his apartment and he carried Marci into what Sinclair assumed was his bedroom, and kicked the door closed.

Sinclair and Tweedledumber were still standing in the elevator. They could hear the moans coming from behind the closed door. Tweedledumber was looking at her, not with desire but slightly bored, like he'd gotten the booby prize.

She was so numb, then angry, then in despair, then angry, and wanting to cry, and to be anywhere on the planet but here with this moron. She looked at him, kneeled down on the floor, unzipped his pants, and shocked the shit out of him. She gave him a blowjob.

When she woke up the next morning in her own bed, she realized she had slept on top of the covers in her clothes and with one boot still on. She awakened in terrible pain. She tried to get her boot off but she couldn't, it was too excruciating. She would have to cut it off. She hobbled down the stairs and limped into the kitchen to get the shears.

"What are you doing?" T.J. was standing in the doorframe, watching Sinclair trying to cut her boot off.

"I'm cutting my boot off."

"I can see that, but why are you cutting your boot off?"

"Because I can't pull it off."

T.J. walked over to help and Sinclair, flinching, stuck her foot into her mother's lap. When T.J. tried to pull it off Sinclair screamed in pain.

"What did you do to yourself?"

"I think I sprained it when I was dancing with Marci last night."

"And you didn't stop dancing on it?"

"No. It didn't hurt."

T.J. cut the boot off. It was a swollen mess. She gave Sinclair aspirins, wrapped her ankle in ice, and drove her to the doctor.

Sinclair was in a walking cast and on crutches for six weeks. No good deed goes unpunished, she thought, lying in bed miserable and in pain.

* * *

Why do you do this to me?

Do what to you?

Give me too much information about Sinclair.

This isn't being written for you, Howard. The readers need to know.

Fuck the readers. That's who you really care about, isn't it?

Howard, if I didn't deeply care about all of you, and you in particular, I wouldn't even be writing this book.

I don't feel cared for. I feel persecuted. Punished.

How are you going to fix anything if you don't learn about what's broken?

Can't we skip to the part where that's already happened? All fixed. Happily ever after.

I'll give you a hint. No fairy tale ending, but something like happily ever after.

As in, looks like happiness, smells like happiness, must be happiness?

Haha. Yes.

Okay. Let's get back to Fire Island.

Don't shoot the messenger.

What the hell are you talking about?

* * *

Since T.J. had invited Cherie to Fire Island, Howard had not been happy. T.J. told him, "So invite one of your own

115

friends." He had plenty of pals he could ask, but his closest friends didn't like being around him and T.J. The possibility of their fighting was not the most relaxing way to spend social time. Being trapped on Fire Island with them? Uh-uh. So, going into the weekend, T.J. was happy, Howard was pissed, and Sinclair was tense.

There was only one photo from that trip, taken by Cherie, of the three of them on the ferry over. T.J. had her eyes closed and was blowing a kiss at the photographer, Howard was squinting, his tight lips tugging down in the corners, and Sinclair was looking away from the camera, wearing dark sunglasses, looking toward the horizon.

He was just about to walk into the cottage after coming back from the beach in the dark when he heard Cherie saying, "Why don't you leave him already?"

He could see them in the light spill from the house, but they couldn't see him. They were sitting in the screened in front porch bundled up in sweaters, smoking weed. He could smell it. Where was Sinclair? Was she listening to this?

"I know. I know."

"He's a millstone. He's a drag on you. He's a sponge."

"I know I should. I should."

"Jesus, T.J. How long have you been saying that?"

"Forever. For years. It's fucking complicated, Cherie."

"You are what's complicated, my darling. You have no fucking idea what you're doing. Or why."

He turned back to the beach even though he was freezing. He would walk all night if he had to. He wasn't going to sleep next to T.J. after that conversation. That was their arrangement. T.J. came to his bed at night. It was all the dignity he had left. And she always did. When she came home at 2 or 4 a.m. she would silently slip into bed beside him. Sometimes he wouldn't even wake up. Sometimes he would still be awake and she would take his hand. He'd lie there in the dark or early morning light and listen to her softly snore.

In the middle of the night, he woke up shivering. T.J. wasn't in bed. What the hell? He put his slippers on, pulled a sweater from his suitcase and a pair of sweatpants and went to check the thermostat. It was on 68. But the temperature read 32. T.J. and Cherie were putting kindling into the fireplace and adding logs. Sinclair was sitting on the couch, piled under blankets. Of course it was impossible to call anyone at this hour. He also had no idea what to do to check on the heater. His father and brother knew this shit, but he'd never learned. He'd lived in apartments all his life. It was the landlord's problem.

He walked up behind them, saying, "Okay this is what we're going to do. Let's pull the mattresses and blankets from our beds and we'll all sleep in front of the fire." He put a false cheerfulness in his voice, implying this would be fun.

T.J., Cherie, and Sinclair seemed reluctant to leave the little bit of warmth that was just starting to generate from the fire.

"Can you do it, Daddy?" Sinclair whined. "I'm so cold. My room is an icebox."

"C'mon Sinclair. We'll all help each other. It'll go faster."

"We should all just cuddle together in one bed for the body heat," T.J. said.

"No!" Was she fucking kidding?!

"Well, this is awkward," Sinclair mumbled, but she got up

and followed Howard into her bedroom.

The mattress arrangements were Cherie's twin on one end, Sinclair's mattress next to hers, and T.J. and Howard's mattress at the other end. Nobody could sleep. They were miserable.

"This is fun," he said.

"Tons," Sinclair said.

"It's like camping."

"Not quite," T.J. said.

"More like a natural disaster," Cherie chimed in.

Howard was so pissed off that Cherie was there. Forced intimacy with his wife's lover. *This* was going to be a conversation when they got home. It was only because things had been so tense before T.J. came up with this brilliant weekend idea that he didn't protest when Cherie was foisted on him. Once more he was the odd man out. Even Sinclair betrayed him by liking Cherie. And after what he'd overheard earlier that night...

The only light in the room came from the fireplace; the only sound was the crackle and pop of the logs. All of them had flipped onto their stomachs, propped up on their elbows and hands, watching the fire. The October wind whipped around the house, creating creaks and groans and the flapping of loose things hitting wood. No streetlight. It was the darkest dark, primordial. He was the only man and this was his tribe. He was the protector. Wasn't it he that thought of the mattresses and huddled his charges around the life-giving fire? Where was his spear if any marauding animals came their way? He smiled to himself.

"I want to continue the conversation Cherie and I were

having before."

Surely not the one *he'd* overheard, Howard thought, his blood pressure rising.

"What were you talking about?" Yes, he was a brave man. He approved of himself.

"Rape."

"Really, T.J.? You want to talk about it with Sinclair here?"

Sinclair let out a groan and collapsed her arms, burying her face in the pillow.

"Yes, why not? Sinclair is about to go off to college..."

"Yeah, in two years..."

"And she needs to know about this stuff. She needs to be prepared for the world. Not just about academic subjects."

She had a point. He couldn't argue with that.

T. J. took his silence as agreement. "Okay, Cherie, tell them what you were telling me."

Cherrie sat up and crossed her legs with her ankles resting on her inner thighs in a yoga position. Means she's in good shape, he thought. She can probably bend like a pretzel. He also noticed her curly, red hair glowing in the firelight. She looked like a religious painting. She could have been a pagan Naiad. Or, if Jesus were a woman, she could have been Jesus.

Cherie pulled the blanket over her shoulders and wrapped herself in it. The problem with fires was that only part of you could be warm at any one time. That's why you had to turn meat when you cooked it. He'd never thought about that before. He had no reason to consciously ever think about it. He felt like he just discovered fire. Or electricity. Or, the wheel. He also felt like laughing, but controlled himself. Really, this desire was just his nervous tic. And, if he did laugh, he'd be drawn and quartered. He would find out what it was like to be turned in a fire.

"I was telling T.J. about this young woman I knew when I was working in the Psych department at Vanderbilt. She was a senior and would be graduating that spring. We really liked each other. She joked around a lot, which made the tedium of the job more bearable. She came into work one morning and said to me, 'If I tell you something, you promise you won't tell a soul?' Does anybody ever say anything but 'yes' to that?"

Sinclair smiled. She was now lying on her side facing Cherie, her head propped up and resting on her palm.

T. J. was also looking at Cherie, but without any discernable expression.

He was noticing how the firelight turned their faces the golden color of autumn leaves.

"Then this young woman told me that she had been in her Professor's office the night before. She was delivering a book back to him that he'd lent her. They were just talking like normal, when he said, 'Close the door, please. There's something I want to tell you that's confidential.' She did as he asked.

"He got up from his desk, walked over to her, leaned in, and whispered in her ear. She didn't repeat what he said. She didn't need to, because the next thing she told me was that he raped her."

"What? Oh, my God," Sinclair said, sitting up.

"Yes," Howard said, "raped by her professor. This is just what I want Sinclair to hear!"

"This shit happens on college campuses, Howard. It happens with men you trust. Why shouldn't Sinclair know this?"

"Yeah, scare the shit out of her before she even gets there."

"Don't treat me like a baby. You can't protect me, Daddy."

It wasn't lost on him that she called him 'Daddy.'

Howard turned back to Cherie. "What did you say to her? What did she do about it?"

"She did nothing, Howard. She told me the story, very matter-of-factly, like this hadn't bothered her in the least. She wasn't shaking or crying, or acting like a rape victim."

"At least, not like how we expect a rape victim to act," added T.J.

"Right, she was in shock, shut down. I begged her to tell me who the teacher was. She absolutely refused to."

"Why wouldn't she?" Howard was exasperated. Pained that Sinclair was hearing this. Pained for the young woman, and even worse, perhaps, feeling an angry helplessness.

"Why?" It was Cherie's turn to get angry. "Because he was famous in his field and she needed a letter of recommendation from him, that's why."

"Well, what about you? What did you do?"

I argued with her. I told her, if he'd done this to her, he would do it again, maybe had already done this to other women students. She wouldn't budge. She wouldn't give me his name. She wouldn't let me report it."

"And that's what Cherie and I were discussing before this evening's ice age hit. We were discussing the different reasons for why."

"No courage," Howard said. "Or self-interest trumps everything."

"What?!" T.J.'s eyes opened wide, gleaming in the firelight, looking demonic in that moment.

His lack of sympathy shocked even him. All he could think about was Sinclair away at college. He wanted this woman to model all the right things to do, the best practices of raped womanhood...for Sinclair's sake...for his own sake. He wanted to believe there were protections, rules, a rational order: report, capture, punishment. Prisons were too good for rapists. Why should tax payers house and feed them? If you simply cut off their balls, problem solved.

He also felt embarrassed and foolish. He was completely ignorant about such things. The legal system made as much sense as the world in a Kafka novel, which of course reflected the real world. When he was older, maybe ten, eleven, and then in his teens, when he didn't know something, or he would fuck up, his mother would shame him by saying, "So, you're not such a genius after all."

"That's right," Cherie was saying to him, "no courage, self-protective, and why the fuck not? She knew no one would believe her."

Smarting from the contempt in her voice, he got louder, more emphatic, as if his words served as proofs in this argument that he knew he couldn't win. He was just flailing. Needing to be right.

"But there are places to report on campus, and she would get help, and maybe others would come forward. What about the police?"

"What are you talking about, Howard? People would suspect she was making this up, think she was crazy perhaps; blame the victim."

"And don't you get it?" T.J.'s turn to attack. "She needed

his letter of recommendation. The blessing of the Pope, the validation from the God on Mount Olympus. She'd be risking her career..."

Cherie was nodding her head in agreement, looking at T.J., but saying to him, "His power over her, compounded by the system's power over her. She consented to keep quiet."

"But that's WRONG! Cherie, you should have reported it, if the girl wouldn't."

"And said what?" Her eyes were fully on him and her mouth curling into a smile was more cutting than her tone of voice could have been.

He realized what an idiotic thing that was to say. He had left being rational behind.

T.J. jumped back in, "And did you know, Howard, that of every thousand rapes, nine-hundred-and-ninety-four perpetrators walk free?"

It was The Lesbian Liberation Front against The Man. How did he get to be, "The Man"? He was on their side.

"Where did you get that statistic?"

"Oh, so, you don't believe me?"

Howard had just opened his mouth to respond, and in that space, in that small moment of silence they heard, "She was just scared."

They all looked at Sinclair. She was crying. "Don't be mad."

T.J. moved closer to Sinclair and touched her arm, her face tight, her eyes frightened.

"I lied about the night I didn't come home."

Howard felt his scalp tingle; his heart skipped as he jumped up and moved next to Sinclair. Their daughter was sandwiched between them. Sinclair was trembling.

"You saved me, Daddy," she whispered.

"What?" Howard asked, utterly confused.

"Tell us from the beginning, Sinclair." T.J. squeezed her hand. "It's okay."

She told them about the masturbator on the train and about the bookstore incident when Bogen asked her to model, and how creepy Bogen became later after the group left, and then how scary he'd become when she asked for the money and he lunged for her.

"Dad, I heard your voice in my head saying, 'Kick him in the nuts, Sinclair!' And I did. As hard as I could." She was crying and gulping air. Cherie got up and found a tissue in her bag and handed it to Sinclair, then sat down beside T.J.

"Shhhh. Shhhh," T.J. said. She put her arm around Sinclair's shoulders, crossing over the top of Howard's arm wrapped around her. He was rocking Sinclair gently. The three of them rocked. "It's okay, baby. You're okay, Rosie."

Cherie reached both arms around T.J. and put one hand on Sinclair's back and her other hand patted Sinclair's leg. Everyone held Sinclair.

This was his tribe, his family; the heat and comfort of their bodies formed a human security blanket. Tonight, they were safe around the fire, keeping the predators at bay.

DR. GLICK

Howard was pacing around Dr. Glick's office, too upset to sit still.

"She could have been raped!"

"Yes."

"Or killed!"

"Yes."

"What am I supposed to do with that?!"

"What you're doing right now."

"You know, I went to the bookstore to find him. This happened to Sinclair six months ago. He was no longer working there."

"Howard, can you sit down, please?"

Howard stopped pacing and sat down heavily.

"Howard, you can't protect her."

"When she said she heard my voice in her head, and said

that I saved her..." He choked back a sob.

"You did the right thing. You comforted her. You loved her."

"Yes, but I feel impotent, like I have no balls."

"What would you like to do? Kill him?"

"Yes."

"Of course you do, but you wouldn't do that. That's not who you are."

"Really? Who am I? Who do you think I am? Because Cherie and T.J. attacked me, making me feel like I was an asshole. But I was right, I know I was right." He looked into Glick's kind eyes.

"I see a good man, a loving man who cares about his wife and daughter more than his own happiness, more than what conventions dictate."

Glick leaned forward in his chair, resting his elbows on his thighs, his hands loosely clasped, maintaining eye contact. "You have a model of what love and family should look like. And more importantly, what you do and don't deserve. You resist your life. You compare it to what you should have, should have had, still want. You won't be happy, Howard, until you let that go."

"You've changed the subject."

"Yes, I did, because there's nothing you can do about keeping your daughter safe in the world. And look what a good father you are. She had you to thank for knowing what to do in that situation."

Howard considered that. It wasn't enough, but Glick had a point.

"But, how do you let go? How do you stop worrying, or

being driven crazy?"

"It's a choice you make."

That answer made him feel nuts.

"Okay, how?"

He folded his arms across his chest. Glick's eyes flickered away from his face, taking the gesture in. He smiled slightly at the challenge.

"Look, your fear about your daughter doesn't change anything. Your anxiety is not about her, it's about you. It is something like belief. You project your belief onto the world, and you experience it like its real. It's not. No amount of worrying about Sinclair is going to change what happens to her. You don't have that power."

That made him smirk. "That's true."

"I want you to refocus."

"On what?"

"I want you to count all the things you do have in your life, the things that are real. You tell me. And there will be no, "buts." We already know the negative side of the list. Tell me the positive things on that list."

He felt a tremendous amount of resistance at this request. He had to talk himself into staying in his seat and not just walking out the door.

He sighed and sat back against the chair, uncrossed his arms and put his palms on the tops of his thighs.

"I have a family. I'm not alone. My daughter loves me. I live in a beautiful house. I don't have to worry about money. We have more than enough. We have food and comforts. We take vacations. I have a lot of independence. I get to make music and write. I'm not a wage slave. I get to watch my daughter grow up. We are all healthy."

Howard paused.

"What else, Howard? Go on."

His voice lowered. "My wife sleeps with me." He swallowed hard, feeling his eyes water, and quickly rubbed them with the palms of his hands.

"She always comes back to me."

"What else, Howard?" Glick said gently.

"My wife will take my hand to tell me she's there, that she wants to be in bed with me. She is so comforted by holding my hand that she's able to fall asleep."

"How does that make you feel when that happens, Howard?"

"Lucky. Loved."

Glick stayed silent, letting that sink in. It was astonishing that these words, in this session, were coming out of his mouth.

"These are the moments that form connection, Howard, that are the peace agreements in the conflicts. The things we offer each other to be able to go on. You feel deprived of a feast. You want more. It's not wrong to want more, but maybe happiness, or at the very least contentment, might be yours if you could celebrate what's offered. You might also find out that reframing your point-of-view will be a gift to your family, and you may be surprised by their offering you much more."

"I can kind of hold onto what you're saying for a few moments, but then an internal voice says that it's settling, that it would be me lying all the time."

"Change is hard, right? Look, think about the fact that we once believed the Earth is flat, but then new knowledge, verified by actual, repeatable experience, created a new conclusion. We discovered that the earth is not flat even though our perception, our beliefs, were precisely that for centuries."

"You're telling me that I have old beliefs that are false, that are misperceptions of reality. And I think they're evidence-based. I think your analogy sucks. Life isn't measurable like a scientific fact."

"Do you think people can change, Howard?"

"Not sure."

"Then why are you here?"

"Because I hope they can."

"Because you hope you can."

"Yes, but all I'm hearing is your telling me that I should just accept my lot in life. Be grateful for what I have."

"That's one interpretation. Think about it, Howard."

* * *

Well, that surprised me.

You make me write things that surprise even me, Howard. Also, I've noticed that whenever something emotional happens, you start talking to me. It just cuts off whatever feeling there was. We go right back up into my head.

So, Miss Author, why do you do it?

I don't know. I guess it makes me uncomfortable.

Why?

I don't know why.

You need to see a therapist.

I do see a therapist.

Is it doing any good?

Not really.

Is his name Dr. Glick?

Ha-ha! Good one.

Can I change the subject?

Okay.

Remember how in the beginning of the story, I asked you to give me a happy memory?

Yes.

And you did?

Yes.

Well, I'm asking again. I need that.

Ok, Howard. Let's jump two years ahead to 2001.

God, now I'm even older.

Yes, you're fifty-five.

Jesus, that makes Sinclair almost eighteen. She'll be leaving home. I don't think I can take it. Not after what just happened.

That's why we're going to a happy time.

* * *

Ever since the family started living in New Jersey, he tried booking more gigs for the band at the Shore, and Maxwell's in Hoboken. When their lead singer had to quit they hired a woman named Solange. Her jazz instincts made their old songs sound fresh. Her vocals were a sexy prowl, confident and knowing. She reminded him of Peggy Lee. She gave them fever.

"What does Solange mean?" Howard asked.

He was sitting with her after their set. He hadn't really had a chance to talk to her. Besides, he shied away from women these days. He didn't have the confidence he once had before T.J. Now women just reminded him that he felt neutered. Dr. Glick, of course, would counter that argument, but he didn't want Glick in his head right now, he wanted to look at Solange and listen to her soft, accented English. He'd always wanted to have a woman speak French to him in bed, to murmur, "Je t'aime" in his ear. Did Jamaicans speak French? That was Haitians, right? He knew nothing about Haiti or Jamaica aside from travel posters for tourism and the fact they'd been exploited and were poor.

"My mother told me, Solange means dignified, but it also means sun angel."

"That fits."

"Which part?"

"Both."

"So you see me as a dignified sun angel?"

"Definitely."

He was trying to figure out how old she was. Black skin didn't age like white skin. He'd known black women in their sixties who looked like they were forty.

"How old are you?" He softened his bluntness with the incredulity in his tone of voice. He could have been carding her to make sure she was drinking age.

She smiled. "One hundred."

"No, really. How old are you?"

He never would have been this direct before life with T.J., who was unfiltered. Painful as this could be, he actually admired it. Glick would have said that real honesty wasn't cruel; it wasn't delivered like a punch to the jaw.

"Guess."

Solange was looking at him curiously. He didn't exactly know the full import of what her expression meant. Instant, non-verbal understanding came with intimacy. Only a cat owner knows the different meanings of meow. It was actually what made beginnings so heady, the uncertainty and projection, the not knowing. But with intimacy came another possibility. For T.J., familiarity bred contempt.

Actually, he hated when women asked you to guess their age. Men always had to err on the younger side or risk insulting the woman.

He studied her skin, eyes, neck, and hands.

"I have no idea. You could be in your late thirties. Early forties."

"Because you just flattered me, I'll tell you the truth. I'm fifty-seven."

She was two years older than him!

"There's no way anyone could tell that."

She smiled, apparently used to this. "Good genes."

"What about me?" Stupid question. Why was he setting himself up for a kick-me?

She looked at him for a moment, and then said, "You're two years younger than me."

"What?! How did you know?"

"I'm a Sun Angel, remember? I see all and know all."

"C'mon. Seriously, who told you my age?"

"Myles, your bandmate. When he was interviewing me, I was interviewing all of you. I asked lots of questions. I wanted to make sure no one was a junkie, or a wife-beater."

"I'm impressed. Very professional. Very business-like."

"No, I'm just smart. And experienced."

"So what else do you know about me?"

"I know you're married and have a teenage daughter."

"Wow. I guess I have to ask Myles for the dirt on you."

"You can ask me."

"Are you married?"

"No."

"Any children?"

"One son. He's married with his own children and lives in California."

"Raised him by yourself?"

"There's a white assumption. Single black mother, unmarried, raises son alone."

"Sorry. It's just that you said you weren't married."

"Now. I'm not married now."

He nodded his head, then looked at her with a teasing smile. "But your husband wasn't the father."

She started to look offended, but then caught on. "Are you always an asshole?" She laughed.

"Pretty much."

He liked her.

He started sticking around after their sets. He was actually flirting with her. How long had it been since he'd done that? It felt good, reclaiming this discarded part of himself, like a retired comic hoping for a successful comeback. Unless he was completely clueless, she seemed to be responding. She was easygoing and playful with all his bandmates, but he wanted to think, that with him, she was a bit more.

One night, after their last set, it started to pour: one of those bone-chilling, late September rains.

"Let me drive you home."

"Really? I live in Manhattan. Won't it be completely out of your way?"

"Sure."

She smiled. There was an immediacy and intimacy when she looked at him. Because she hit a nerve, he looked away. He'd been obsessed with T.J. for so long, he was amazed he could see another woman in this way. And to desire a woman who was kind and not making him work hard? Not that he was pursuing her. He had no agenda. His attraction was both free floating and like a compass pointer. He stopped analyzing and just allowed himself the experience.

He felt happily cocooned in the car with the rain pelting down, the swoosh of the wipers, the haloed glow of street lamps, how empty the streets were. His car radio was broken so they drove in silence. It wasn't an awkward silence. She was tired. It had been a long day. He was tired too, but his nervous excitement about being alone with her had emerged as soon as she'd said yes.

"When I was a little girl a terrible hurricane hit Jamaica. I was terrified by the water rising, the trees bending their heads to the ground, the relentless wind. That was scary enough, but worse was the helplessness of my parents, the losses to us, and everyone. I have never been that afraid again. I don't like rain."

He realized that he was having a very different experience than Solange. It was always sobering, this realization, no matter how many times he experienced it in life; it caught him up short.

"I can understand that. I've never lived through something

that horrific. It amazes me that people do. That you did. You survived. Here you are in the car next to me. And now I'm even happier about it because I can get you home safely."

She had stopped looking out the window and was looking at him. Then she took his hand. It was so unexpected. It gave him something like the happiness he felt when T.J. took his hand in bed. She squeezed, then let it go.

They didn't have sex that night. They didn't have sex for a couple of months. It was a slow burn of a courtship. In the old days, sex would have come first and then the getting to know someone, if that even developed. They talked a lot instead.

He told her:

"T.J. and I don't have sex."

"I'm not even sure about performing with another woman."

"I need to be able to trust you."

"I don't want to get hurt."

She told him:

"I'm skeptical about the motives of a white man."

"I need to be able to trust you."

"I feel ambivalent about getting involved with a married man."

"I don't want to get hurt."

He asked her:

"Why did the marriage end?"

She asked him:

"Why do you stay with T.J.?"

But really, the conversations were not important. Or not nearly as important as, "You were wonderful. I could listen to you sing all night."

She touched his cheek with the palm of her hand and smiled into him. He felt happy all the way down.

She made Jamaican beef patties. T.J. never cooked for him. She rubbed his neck and shoulders. She smelled wonderful.

He wrote a song for her. He sang it to her at her apartment by candlelight, after a glass of wine. That was the night she kissed him. They kissed and nothing more.

He thought about her all the time.

She touched him on the arm. He touched the small of her back.

These were exquisite, excruciating weeks.

The answers to, 'Who are you?' had little to do with what they said.

And then during a freak snowstorm when he drove her home and knew he couldn't make it back to Jersey, she insisted he stay. "You'll sleep with me."

"You mean?"

She said, "We'll see."

She laughed; she laughed like they were sharing a good joke, one that he wouldn't be the butt of, and then went into the bathroom, returning to bed naked. He was already under the covers, his clothes, removed hastily, were a small pile on the floor. He watched her walk toward him without any shyness or self-consciousness. She was body-proud. She knew she was beautiful, but she couldn't really know how beautiful she was to him. She lifted the sheets and slid into bed, waiting for him. He enfolded her. He loved her slowly. She allowed him time. When she moaned she was instructing him wordlessly: yes, more of this, yes, do that. They looked at each other, at first with surprise and then with lust. They discovered they could please each other. Their bodies and appetites were a fit. His old confidence came flooding back.

They made love three times, to his astonishment. It was like the old days. He felt twenty years younger. He had never felt gratitude toward a woman after sex before, but he did now. The last time they made love was in the early morning, and then he called T.J.

* * *

Thank you. But I wish you had described the sex.

I've done that before, written graphic sex scenes, in another novel I wrote.

Was I in it?

No.

You have other male characters?

Yes.

Well, that makes me feel weird.

Sorry, Howard.

There's all kinds of faithlessness.

Jealousy is a cruel emotion.

I used to be jealous of T.J.'s lovers. But then I became numb.

Maybe you're just tolerant and open-minded.

Now you sound like Glick.

You see? You've done it again, Howard. Cut away from the emotion of the story.

Yes, why did you do it this time?

I'm stalling.

Oh, fuck.

* * *

He lay next to Solange as he talked to T.J. on the phone. He wanted her to hear.

Yes, he was stuck because of the storm. He was at Solange's. He'd be home as soon as the streets were plowed.

Then T.J. said, uncharacteristically, "Drive safely." Of all the things she could have said, this was one that unnerved him.

When he came home a day later, T.J. greeted him with a glass of wine.

"Where's Sinclair?"

"Out at a friend's house."

"Are you sure?"

"What? We're never going to trust her again?"

"Maybe."

T.J. plopped down on the couch and swung one leg over the stuffed armrest, her slipper dangling as she moved her foot up and down.

"You're looking pretty happy."

"Am I? I guess I am."

Actually, he was feeling nervous, like he was being

spooked. But there was also the feeling of *Fuck off, T.J.*

"I like it when you're happy."

Howard had been standing with his coat on. He put the untouched glass of wine down on a table, removed his coat and hung it up.

"I don't make you happy."

This, he thought, was a curious lead-in. When was the last time T.J. initiated a conversation, as opposed to an argument, about him? Or them?

Howard picked up his glass of wine and sat in the stuffed chair facing the couch. Their house was fairly conventionally decorated and had old-fashioned furniture designed for comfort. The little he knew about the ultra modern home T.J. grew up in gave him some understanding of her desire for its antithesis. He had little to say about the décor, nor did he care. The house was more than he ever dreamed of, or ever intended to live in. It felt warm, cozy, broken-in, and was the most conventional thing about their lives.

He smiled at her. "No, T.J., for the most part you don't make me happy. Sometimes, you make me happy. When you want to."

"You don't make me happy either, Howard. But I love you."

That was a shocker. Her saying it.

"You have a very weird way of showing it."

She sighed. "You're very annoying, Howard."

"You didn't used to think so."

She thought for a moment. "That's true. In the beginning, I saw that you could drive me crazy, but other parts of you intrigued and impressed me, and made me feel safe."

"I make you feel safe?"

"Yes."

"Why?"

But he knew why. He stayed. He accepted her for who she was, at his own expense. He still loved her, for no fathomable or good reason he could think of. But he was falling in love with Solange, so maybe he didn't have to stay. Yet he couldn't give up Sinclair.

"I don't entirely know why."

"That makes two of us."

She stopped dangling her foot and sat up straight on the couch. She sipped her wine. He didn't say anything. He waited. He wanted an answer.

"Try."

He recognized that furrow between the brows that signaled her tension and entrapment. She sighed. And looked at him. "We are family."

Yes, we are family, he thought, disappointed.

Sinclair opened the front door and walked in, pulled off her boots and gloves and hung up her coat. When she took off her hat Howard still reacted with surprise. She had recently cut off even more of her beautiful hair and was now wearing a choppy short cut that made her look boyish—something like T. J. when he first met her, but without the two-tone dye job.

"You two look cozy."

She smiled and plopped down next to T.J., who put her arm around her shoulders and pulled her closer. Another uncharacteristic gesture. Not that T.J. never did this, but it was rare. He looked at the tableau of his wife and daughter and had the thought that this was spontaneously staged by T.J. for his benefit—a real photo opportunity, a Hallmark card moment.

And he resented her for the fact that it worked.

Washing his hands before dinner, he thought about Solange. Putting his dish in the sink, he thought about Solange. Looking at his daughter, he thought about Solange. In between every other frame of reality, he thought about Solange.

In bed, T.J. rolled over and faced him. "Want to have sex?" she asked.

"No," he said

"No? You never turn me down."

"You never ask."

"First time for everything."

"I know what you're doing, T.J."

"You do?"

He wasn't going to say it.

Then she said, "I broke up with Cherie."

This was a big surprise. Cherie and she had lasted longer than any of T.J.'s relationships. They'd moved to Jersey because of Cherie. He hated Cherie. Despite himself, there was some satisfaction in learning this.

"Why did you break up?"

"It was time."

Typical T.J.

"Goodnight," he said, rolling away from her.

"Goodnight," she said. He felt her kiss on his naked back.

* * *

Howard booked an out-of-town gig for the band. They'd be gone for a week in Nashville. When he told T.J., all she said was, "Have fun." Then, as he was about to walk out the bedroom door to leave, she said, "Wait a minute…"

She was wearing an oversized t-shirt and nothing else. She walked over to where he stood, grabbed the back of his neck, pulled his head toward her and kissed him hard on the mouth. At the same time, she took his hand and rubbed his fingers into her vagina. Then she released him, turned and walked off into the bathroom.

He was stunned, angry. And hard. What a manipulative game-player. What a bitch.

He wanted to follow her. T.J.'s vagina was one of the top ten reasons he'd married her.

He opened the door and left. In the car he smelled his fingers as he drove to pick up Solange.

"What, will these hands ne'er be clean?" he thought, running his soapy hands under the water at the first gas station he could find. Great. Now he identified with Lady Macbeth.

He didn't know what he felt guiltier about: betraying Solange with his desire for T.J., or betraying himself with his desire for T.J.

SINCLAIR

Sinclair walked into the kitchen after she came home from school and opened the refrigerator. T.J. was sitting at their large farmhouse kitchen table looking at prints she'd made.

"Hi, Sinclair."

"Hi," she said, her back turned to T.J.

Sinclair opened a milk carton and considered guzzling it out of the carton, but T.J. might look up and yell at her. She poured herself a glass, then opened a cupboard door and began rooting around until she found the cookies she wanted.

Standing and leaning on the kitchen counter, she looked over at T.J.

"Where's dad?"

"He's on the road with Solange."

"You mean with the band."

"Yes, with the band."

"Why did you say, 'with Solange'?"

T.J. put down the print in her hand and looked at Sinclair, who had stopped munching her cookie and was looking at her mother.

"You *are* my daughter, aren't you?" A corner of T.J.'s mouth twitched up into a half smile.

"Are you kidding? *This* is how I find out?"

T.J. sighed. "You must have known."

"How could I know?"

"Because of how different he's been."

"I didn't think about it. I just assumed that you two were in one of your cycles where you were getting along better than usual. I never imagined him cheating. You're the one who has the affairs. Not him."

"Why can't he have an affair?"

"Because he's a better person than you are."

"It has nothing to do with that."

"Is he leaving you?"

"You mean us. Is he leaving us?"

"Thanks. Spoken like a truly caring parent. 'Sinclair, this is between Mommy and Daddy. We both still love you. Daddy isn't leaving you, Sinclair. He's leaving Mommy.' Why is this family so fucking abnormal!"

"Every family is abnormal in their way," T.J. said calmly.

The milk and cookies forgotten, Sinclair stalked over to the table and sat down hard on a chair facing her mother.

"Why don't you talk to your parents, Mom?" This was a good way to get even.

T.J.'s face tensed, her lips compressed. "It's none of your business."

Sinclair screamed, *"WHY DON'T YOU TALK TO YOUR PARENTS*?!"

"You really want to know why? Okay. But, you won't like it, Sinclair." It was her turn to look angry, to feel threatened.

Good, Sinclair thought. Now they were both scared.

"It's not going to support your theory about normal families."

"Just tell me."

T.J.

Growing up, T.J. knew that Sarah would easily have thrown her under a bus to get Ross back. But, as the marriage eroded, Sarah stopped caring about the loss of Ross. She became more mask-like, performance-based, and lacquered. It was hard to say if this wouldn't have happened even without the arrival of T.J. By witnessing the marriage up close and personal, it was, in T.J.'s opinion, doomed anyway. Her parents were narcissists—Sarah was obsessively self-centered and Ross was an arrogant charm boy. Each of them expected to be adored. The competition between them would have eventually worn thin. T.J. had simply hastened their estrangement.

By the time she was a teenager the only passion in the family came from her emotional outbursts. She was the inflamed, hot, expressive, sexy, larger-than-life noise in the house, the uncontainable mess. It wasn't until her twenties that she'd rein herself in and learn to be cool like her mother. It was less painful than always leading with her chin.

One Saturday afternoon in late August, T.J. was in the garage, about to drag the garbage cans down the driveway to the curb. She'd finally relented after two hours of intermittent nagging by her mother. When she heard the sound of a motorcycle, she looked out the open garage door. Daddy's home. She watched as his motorcycle came into view and he turned into their driveway. He was wearing a black leather jacket, a motorcycle helmet, and boots. He could have been Marlon Brando. She was wearing shorts, a t-shirt, and sandals. God, he must have been hot. The price paid for being "cool."

He pulled in and parked right next to where she was standing and then turned the noisy beast off. She hated the sound of motorcycles. Still straddling the bike and putting down the kickstand, he sat back and took off his helmet.

"Whatcha up to, kiddo?"

"Nothin'. Mom wanted me to put out the garbage cans."

She could see he was dripping sweat.

"Ya know, I have an idea. Before the school year starts, why don't we go on a vacation together?"

"Yeah?"

"A road trip. We take the bike cross-country."

"What about Mom?"

"I was thinking, just you and me."

Her genuine smile froze into a pretend smile. She was totally creeped out.

"I don't think so," was her flippant answer, reverting to one type of performance in the family drama.

She turned and walked back into the house.

She heard her father dragging the garbage cans down to the street. The scraping set her teeth on edge.

* * *

"I was sixteen," T.J. began.

Sinclair's stomach clenched, seeing the revelation of pain in her mother's eyes. T.J.'s open hand lay on the table, palm up, fingers curled. Impulsively, Sinclair took her hand out of her lap and clasped T.J.'s. A current of fear and sympathy passed between them.

"It was after supper. I was bored. God knows where my mother was. She was probably lying down with one of her headaches. I decided to knock on my father's door. He had his own gabled room, at the top of the stairs.

"Who is it?" he asked.

"It's me," I said.

"Come in, T.J." His voice sounded relieved.

When I opened the door I found him sitting at his desk in a cone of lamplight. There were no windows in his room and the rest of the space fell away into darkness. Whatever he'd been reading was now face down. There was no place to sit except for his lap, or on the twin bed across the room.

"Come, sit down." He patted his knees with both hands.

It made me feel very much like a little girl, like his little girl. No matter what I had witnessed about him over the years, and whatever my judgmental thoughts had been, there was still something very primal about my love for my daddy.

Sitting on his lap, he asked me about school, my friends, and then he said, "What about boys? Do you have a boyfriend?"

"No," I said.

"What about kissing? Have you ever kissed a boy?"

That was weird.

"No." Which was true at that point. I had only kissed a girl.

"Here, let me teach you."

He kissed me on the mouth. He leaned back and looked at me, and I realized I was smiling because I didn't know what I was supposed to do. I was frozen. He kissed me again, but passionately.

"Like this," he whispered. "Do you like this?" When he kissed me once more, I kissed him back. He gave me a squeeze and said, "You're getting the hang of it. I believe you're a natural."

That week, he went out of town on a business trip. Saying nothing to my mother, I packed a bag and left home. That was the last time I ever stepped foot in my parents' house."

"Oh, my God." Sinclair let out her breath. She was gripping her mother's hand.

"So, now you know," T.J. sighed, her voice ragged.

"Did you ever tell your mother?'

"I tried. She didn't want to hear it."

"And your father?"

"After I left, I refused to speak to him."

When I ran away I stayed with a friend for a week and then I went to Greenwich Village. I was living on the streets and then got taken in by an older lesbian. She was in her forties. I fell madly in love with her and for a while it was wonderful. Then she became abusive and sadistic. I was suicidal. Apparently, I'm a survivor, because I got help—therapy, friends—and I went back to school.

My parents gave me money. I asked them to pay for college and to buy me the loft in Soho, and to put it in my name. I have a trust fund, but I've always worked. I haven't communicated with my parents since I married Howard. They don't even know you exist.

"You never told Howard?"

"I never told him. So now you know. Are you glad you know, Sinclair?"

She didn't know what the fuck to say.

* * *

Well, now I know. Jesus Christ.

Yes, Howard, now you know.

I guess I should feel privileged to find out information that my character doesn't have in the story, but instead, it feels awful, because this is my story. This is happening to me, in my life. I can't talk to Sinclair or T.J. about it. I can't even talk to Dr. Glick.

Why not?

Because how would I explain that I know this?

You can talk to me, Howard. We're on the same page.

Are you kidding? You're making a joke?

Sorry. It just slipped out. I think you should go to Nashville with Solange and forget about what you know.

How do I do that?

You go back to being a character in the book.

* * *

Howard woke up from a dream where something bad was happening to Sinclair. He couldn't shake this feeling even as he gained consciousness and tried to hold onto the images in his head. No good. Gone.

Solange was sleeping peacefully beside him in their hotel bed. He felt disoriented and troubled. The Talking Heads' lyric came to mind. "And you may tell yourself, 'This is not my beautiful house!' And you may tell yourself, 'This is not my beautiful wife!'"

Guiltily, he reached for Solange, wanting to feel anchored in the tangible, the real. She sighed and opened her eyes.

"What's the matter?" she asked when she saw his face. Her tone was warm and sympathetic.

He had no earthly idea.

"Just a feeling I have." He began to cry.

He realized that it wasn't the same now that he had broken down in front of Solange and confessed that he felt guilty and worried about Sinclair. It was better. Deeper. Solange had been completely understanding and comforting. He thought she was remarkable. A woman in a class by herself. A stellar human being.

"Howard, I wouldn't have respected you if you didn't feel this way."

"But what does it mean about us?"

They were sitting in Brown's Diner, a Nashville institution where songwriters and musicians had been coming for beers and burgers forever. The only weird thing about being there was that Solange was the only black person in the place. It was okay at Brown's but he realized that being in the South together was awkward, even though it was already two thousand and fucking one. Being that he was a white male, and therefore oblivious, it hadn't really occurred to him that this could be a problem for Solange. It was different when the band performed. The stage and music was a protection for his friends and lover.

But, on lower Broad in downtown Nashville, walking with Solange and holding hands, some redneck in the crowd yelled, "Nigger lover," stunning him. He whipped around, but the tourist crowd was thick on these streets and there was no way to know who it was. While he seethed, Solange remained perfectly cool.

"How can you stand it?" Howard said, having just peered into the reality of her daily life.

"You just do. You don't let it in. Unless there's real danger, you flick off the flies and they return to buzzing around their own shit."

"Well, it's a fucking shit show, isn't it?" he said.

"Yes, it is, but as my mother would say, 'Though I walk through the valley of the shadow of death, I shall fear no evil.'"

"Well, I do fear evil." He put his arm protectively around her waist and pulled her to him as they continued walking down the street.

"Not a great idea," she said, but she leaned into him, smiling to herself.

"I love you," he said. He hadn't said the words before. She didn't say them back, but he looked at her profile and he thought she looked happy.

He noticed a cockroach crawling along the floor at Brown's. He didn't want to call it to Solange's attention. It pretty much killed his appetite. He nursed his beer and didn't eat any more of his burger, which had been tasting great.

"What's the matter? Why aren't you eating?"

"I don't know. I've had enough. You didn't answer my question."

"About us?" Her expression didn't change. She gazed calmly at him. "It's pretty simple, Howard. It means we're not forever, but we have now. For awhile."

"How long is awhile?"

"I don't know. But, I think we'll both know when it's time."

"That sounds like something said when you decide to take a loved one off life support."

She laughed. "It's kinda the same thing. We're on life support right now."

"No miracle cure?" He was wise cracking from being nervous.

She didn't answer.

"What are you thinking, Solange?"

"Don't you really mean, what am I feeling?" She touched his hand with the tip of her finger.

"Yes." She didn't let him get away with a thing.

"I'm feeling lots of things. Sorrow and disappointment. Happiness, sexually opened, appreciated, loved. And also, love for you."

He felt that old thrill when hearing someone who matters saying these words for the first time.

"I love you," he said, for the second time that day, but not the happy 'I love you.' Rather, saying it to reassure and testify.

"Sweet words, Howard, and a sweet feeling. But, beyond right now, it's not enough. I wanted more, you know I did, even when I knew that a happy ending was highly unlikely. The odds were against me—a white man, with a wife and teenage daughter?"

"It happens. It could still happen."

He was pleading now. Not to make her still believe so much as to make them both will a different ending into being. His desire was religious.

"Not likely," she said, sober and practical as always.

No fantasy life for Solange. She took her heartache straight, but the admirable thing to Howard was that it was something absorbed, becoming an addition to self instead of a diminishment. He couldn't fathom how she did it.

"Especially after I got to know you, Howard...I realized..."

"What does that mean?"

"It means that you aren't done with T.J."

"Yes, because of Sinclair."

"Howard."

The way she said his name made him feel ashamed. Why is it everyone knew him better than he knew himself?

"But I don't want to be with T.J."

"Let's just take T.J. out of the picture for a moment. You are never leaving your marriage for another woman, because of Sinclair. At least not until she's grown."

That was true, he realized just then, hearing it said. If he thought of himself as a man who could never know his feelings in any pure, uncontaminated way, this was the exception. His love for Sinclair was simple and straight-arrowed; it had pierced his heart the moment he knew she was alive, just a kick in T.J.'s belly, a shape on the printed ultrasound image. It was in fact the only really immutable thing he'd known in his life.

"Okay, that feels true, but I swear I didn't know this until you."

"Not much of a compliment." But her tone wasn't offended. She was teasing.

"No, no," he rushed to get out the words, "I meant, all these years of remaining faithful for no understandable reason—I had no way to know that I couldn't leave because I was afraid to love anyone else, perhaps couldn't. I thought, maybe something in me had died. Perversely, or self-protectively, putting it on the line was something I was either not interested in, or didn't want to risk. And then I met you and all of that became irrelevant, swept away. I had my answer."

"The answer is: you can't."

It felt like she was looking into him with her serious eyes, eyes that he couldn't look away from, that had drawn him to her since they met.

"No, no, the answer is, I can. You were more compelling than my being fearful. A dignified sun goddess named Solange had called me forth." He grinned, beaming all the good will he had in the world toward her.

"Thank you," she said, and was all she needed to say.

The diner door opened and a small group entered noisily and sat down at a nearby table, breaking the spell. They'd been lucky since they had been practically the only ones in the place the whole time, having arrived at an off-hour.

"Anything else I can get for you folks?" Howard noticed

the waitress eyeballing his half-finished burger.

"I'd like another Bud, please."

The waitress removed Solange's empty plate. "Anything for you, hon?"

She shook her head, no, and as soon as the waitress left, he picked up where they'd left off.

"There's something you said that I want to get back to, something I didn't understand. What does my being white have to do with anything?"

She looked at him, for the first time, like women will look when they think you are an incredibly dense knucklehead, or when they feel like an exasperated parent talking to a know-nothing child.

"Not much between us, when it's just us. We're merely two people who are attracted to each other and love the people we are with each other. But sometimes being white and black gets in the way. I've seen it be a fascination, a distraction, and a false topic. It can also be a giant 'fuck you' to society, and therefore it may only be skin deep."

"But that's only if you don't relate as a real person. Besides, everyone is other."

"You being a white male means there are all kinds of opportunities for me to get hurt, not out of malice, but out of your obliviousness."

"Then you'll educate me."

"You're killing me, Howard." This time he heard the sadness in her voice. "Don't make offers you can't follow through on."

Were those tears in her eyes? Tears for him? Who had ever cried for him? How could he possibly give her up?

"I love that you're still a romantic, Howard, because believe it or not, I am, too. But experience has led me not to believe in permanence. Loving and being attached to someone comes with pain. So, I accept what I have now. I won't live my life not taking risks. I'd rather be heartbroken than never feel intimacy with another person. I told you I felt afraid of getting hurt by you. But, finally, I didn't let that stop me."

"But what if the pain is lifelong?" The calculation of this made him feel bereft.

"All pain is lifelong. We never forget the pain. It's so much harder to remember the joy."

"I can't believe your husband didn't stay with you. How could he have given you up? He was an idiot."

She smiled wryly at that. "You're giving me up, Howard... But I'll tell you who is not giving you up. T.J. is not giving you up. It sounds like she's decided to keep you, after all."

Against his better judgment, he had told Solange about the kiss. Though he didn't report his reaction.

Again, he was dumbstruck about the different responses to a shared experience. While he felt so good this morning, more open and even closer to Solange, she was gaining insight into their relationship being doomed.

"But we're not done, are we?" Howard asked. "This is not our goodbye conversation."

But what could he counter-offer, what was he proposing? That he and Solange go on, like T.J.'s affairs just go on? What a pair they were, he and T.J., as models for a successful adult relationship for their daughter. But Sinclair didn't know, did she, although it couldn't be kept a secret forever. He wished it wouldn't matter. He wished he could dismiss it as cultural convention. But he knew better. Conventions grew out of the need for human protections, and most fundamentally to protect the human heart. What a mess he'd made by wanting something for himself, which didn't alter the truth that Solange was a gift. Why could he never have what he wanted without consequence? Life was so perverse. There was nothing about being alive that made sense. What a useless animal development consciousness was. We create the rules for our own suffering. When he'd read about self-flagellation in *The Confessions of Saint Augustine*, he thought it was curious and aberrant, but now he understood it as a more extreme extension of the judgments and punishments we all inflict on ourselves. Not aberrant at all. Not even Catholic. Just an expression of being human to control the beast within, to contain the ever-threatening animal desires that bring disorder.

He got up and sat down beside Solange in the booth. He took both her hands and looked at her. He thought he might kiss her, but she pulled away just ever so slightly. Not here. Not now.

"No, Howard," she said softly. "It's just the beginning of our end." This time she turned her head away, concealing her expression.

SINCLAIR

She'd sat there stunned while T.J. got up from the table and rinsed her glass in the sink.

"I don't know what to say, Mom."

"I know."

"Are you okay?"

T.J. had her back to her as she stood with her fingers spread on the counter top, her shoulders hunched.

"Yeah. Yeah. Of course I am." She turned around and gave her a forced smile. "It happened a long time ago. It's just new for you. Are you okay?"

Sinclair quickly reconstituted herself to be the okay daughter, the one in the family without problems. Don't impose yourself on this fragile infrastructure.

"Yeah, sure. I don't know. I guess."

She and T.J., mother and daughter, had no language, no

experience with handling such emotional piercings of their world. Sinclair was experiencing a kind of vertigo and felt like she could be the one clinging to the kitchen counter to stay standing. She could not *not* imagine being T.J., and yet it was also unimaginable. She wanted to touch her mother as much as she wanted to flee. She felt like her reaction was insensitive and peculiar. She felt separated and twinned. She was appalled at herself. She was also appalled by her father. She had no one.

"Sinclair," her mother said. "I have a favor to ask." She still kept her distance, remaining standing at the sink, leaning her back against the counter.

"What?" She felt panicky, like her throat was swelling shut. *Imaginary bullshit*, she thought, scolding herself. *Don't be a child. Pull yourself together.*

"I want you to stay at a friend's house tonight."

T.J. had never asked her to do this before.

"Why?" Her terror was back.

"Because I just want you to. Please don't question me."

She was afraid that she may not be able to stand.

"Fine," she managed to say.

The room looked unfamiliar, like someone had replaced it with a lookalike kitchen. She wanted her mother to turn around and comfort her. She wanted her mother to tell her it would be okay.

As she trudged up the steps to her room to call her friend and throw stuff in her backpack, she wondered if she would ever know normal. She wanted Howard. She wanted her Daddy. But now there was a gully of anger that separated them. Maybe this would be the end of having a daddy. He'd become her Father. A man that lived somewhere else and saw her on alternate weekends. She was livid. How could he do that to her? And T.J.'s father? How could he do that to *her*?!

* * *

I don't want to go home.

Howard, you have to go home.

I don't want to see T.J. and, maybe for the first time in my life, I don't want to see Sinclair.

You can't stay with Solange. You're expected. You said you'd be back on Sunday, and Sinclair needs you.

Sinclair will hate me.

Yes, and you will have to allow it. That's what good parents do. They let their children hate them so that they can know you won't stop loving them even as they're being completely awful.

Is this a 20th or 21st century thing?

What do you mean?

Did teenagers in the 1800s do this?

I have no idea.

I bet they didn't. Modern childhood was invented after WWII, because of all the death and displacement, all the orphans. I don't think it was an improvement. I don't think we're kinder, gentler people. The world is still as fucked up.

Too big a topic to argue here, Howard. And you're just stalling to avoid the inevitable.

Not entirely. I'm trying to figure out how I should behave.

Why don't you talk to Glick?

If you insist.

* * *

So there he was again in the nondescript patient chair facing Dr. Glick, angry and confused.

"Do I tell Sinclair my first night back? What if T.J. has told her already? What's the right attitude for me to have? How can I possibly explain? She's seventeen years old. She can't begin to understand."

"I don't think you explain, Howard. You state, and then you listen. She will tell you what you need to say. It's called responding."

"I don't need your sarcasm."

"It wasn't entirely sarcastic." Glick gave Howard one of those wise smiles that irritated him. Who died and gave him all the answers? Maybe seeing Glick was a big mistake.

"It's okay, Howard. Here's the place you can be angry, should be angry."

"Why do I feel patronized?"

"Because a man is telling you to be a man, the good man that you actually are, and you feel instructed. It feels parental."

Howard groaned. But he had to admit, Glick made sense; he wasn't wrong.

"Are you modeling how I should be with Sinclair?"

"Sort of."

"I hate when you're right."

"Nobody likes to feel like they're wrong. But, this doesn't have to do with who's right and wrong. Have I ever made you feel morally judged?"

Howard paused to think about it.

"No."

"I don't believe in that any more than you do."

"That's one reason I see you."

"It's about taking care of Sinclair's feelings. Protecting her."

"Do I have to do this with T.J.?"

"T.J.is a different story. T.J. is a grownup. It's a negotiation. What do you want from T.J.?"

"Probably what I've always wanted from her. To feel loved by T.J."

"She loves you."

"Doesn't matter. I want to feel beloved."

Glick nodded. "That's the negotiation. Hold out for it, Howard. Otherwise giving up Solange will make you bitter in the long run."

"Well, I'm not giving Solange up. Not yet. And it's still not game over. Despite Sinclair, I could still leave. I could be happy with Solange. It would be different. Sinclair would adjust. It would be hard, but other children do it."

He was saying it out loud, testing it, trying to believe it. He sank his head between his hunched shoulders and looked at his hands, turning them over in his lap. He was remembering Sinclair's baby hand gripped around his index finger, surprising him that first time, its own force of nature, holding on for dear life.

"Who am I kidding? She's seventeen. It would be the worst thing to do. But, when I look at my hands, I see they're becoming old man's hands. If not now, when? It's not like you get to love a lot of times in your life."

Glick sucked on his pipe and just looked at Howard

thoughtfully.

"What are you thinking?"

"I was thinking that we always believe that what we have now will be what we'll have later. And that could happen. One possibility, after the drama subsides, and you are happily partnered with Solange, is that you'll become more certain every day that you made the right decision. Or, maybe over time you'll discover things you didn't know about Solange, or that she didn't know about you, and, confoundingly, this will start to replicate the psychological core of your life with T.J. You've just traded out partners who ultimately disappoint you in uncannily similar ways."

"Solange could never be T.J.," he said fiercely.

"No, she'd be another version of your unhappiness."

"Is this the family therapy playbook for survival? A much better tactic to take than using the moral arguments? More effective with someone like me."

Glick chuckled.

"Many people trade partners. They don't kill themselves reflecting about it like I do. They just think they've been un-lucky with their choices. You hear that Allan, who's been mar-ried two times before, married Mildred, and it's now been five years and he's happy and in love. She's the keeper."

"Yes," Glick nodded, "and perhaps without his knowing it, or without sharing his private thoughts with his friends, he had been changing, and refining what he did and didn't want, would and wouldn't accept. Or maybe he got lucky. But there are just as many people you could have married three, four, five times and never found anything lasting, and always felt they made the wrong choices, and that never changed for their entire lives."

"So it's a risk. No guarantees."

"Not ever."

"But the heart wants what the heart wants. I know it's a cliché," Howard said.

"But it's true. Time's up, Howard. Stuff to think about. When do you go home?"

"Tonight."

"Nothing has to be decided tonight. My advice is to stay open, to listen, and to take the pressure off yourself. Just witness, be present. Don't start a fight. That would be taking the easy way out."

On the drive home from Glick's session Howard thought about *Father Knows Best*, an extremely popular, completely impossible, saccharine situation comedy from the 1950s. Nobody had that neat suburban life, ever. It amazed him that this was what people related to. It was the template for an entire generation that always felt like they failed to live up to this image of how American family's behaved, how people lived. It made everyone believe there was something wrong with them and their family. He couldn't imagine what it would have been like to be black, an immigrant, or a Native American watching these shows. The message of exclusion and failure by making comparison had to have been so much worse than his. The defense against it was sneering back, or parodying it. But no matter how dopey or sexist or middle class it was—something to aspire to, or be excluded from—it made you feel bad about your own deprived life. Who wanted that airbrushed life? Americans did!

He pulled into the driveway and sat in the car, procrastinating. He imagined walking through the door and exclaiming, "Honey, I'm home!" and T.J. greeting him in her shirtwaist dress and high heals, with her tasteful, single strand of pearls at her throat. She would lean toward him from the waist up and he would lean down to peck her on the cheek.

"Where's the Princess?"

"Here I am, Daddy!"

And he would bend over to kiss the top of Sinclair's head.

When he actually opened the door and hung up his stuff, he yelled, "Hello? Anybody home?"

The house was dead quiet. "Hello?" he repeated, walking down the hall, past the kitchen.

"I'm down here, Howard."

He walked down the basement steps toward T.J.'s darkroom. The door was open, so he walked in.

"Hi," she said, in the middle of hanging wet prints above their chemical baths.

He stood a few feet away, looking at the row of prints.

"Wow. These are gorgeous, T.J."

"You think so?"

She was still stretched with her arms above her head, fastening the last shot to the line.

"This is new work."

"Yes, I'm collaborating with a Japanese artist I met. I fell in love with what she is doing."

Finished, T.J. turned to him, smiling, her eyes alive with excitement.

It had been awhile since T.J. had bothered to share her

work in its developmental phase, eager for his opinion. They used to have long discussions in the old days. She always wanted him to be super-critical, but would easily bristle. He had to learn to talk about her work so that it wouldn't turn into a fight. But the best times, when the discussions were lively and philosophical, and they became cozy and companionable, he would watch her unfold. T.J. in bloom, like a rare flower that only opened in moonlight.

And now, there was that girl again standing in front of him, eager for more of what he could offer, but also not the same girl, because she was confident and mature, and damn, that made her sexy.

"I'll tell you what I'm seeing," he said, "and then you explain to me how this is possible."

"Yes."

As she watched him absorbing the images, he imagined her seeing more in his face than he knew he was revealing. T.J. processed the world through her eyes. She was the least psychologically analytical creature: the complete opposite of him.

The first black and white in the series was of a woman in a dimly-lit hallway, naked, with her back to the viewer. The skin on her torso had various patches of mottled flesh, while others took on a metallic patina, much like copper when exposed to the elements.

"I see the figure of a young beautiful female body that is decaying," he said. "There is nothing ugly about this. The image is eerie, but not supernatural, though it is unreal. It plays tricks with your perception."

He looked at her. "I can't tell what I'm looking at exactly, because it looks like a living person."

"How do you feel looking at it?"

He wanted to smile because this was a question he'd taught her.

"It makes me feel melancholy and spooked. I feel moved. To me it's full of sadness and loss, the kind that haunts you after waking up from a dream."

"Oh, my God, Howard. Could you write that down for me?"

She went over to him and, without pressing her body against his, she rested her head on his chest.

"Thank you," she said.

He couldn't touch her. He wanted to put his arms around her, but he couldn't. She got the message and stepped away.

He turned his attention to the next images in the series. In each shot, the figure became more eroded. It was geological, like rock layers revealed. It was the exposure of history, hidden and lost, made physical.

The last shot was of the figure shattered on the ground in pieces with identifiable parts of the head and body in shards. It was painful to look at. A terrible destruction. A violation.

"Okay, now tell me what I'm looking at."

"A female Japanese sculptor makes these figures and then decomposes them slowly in chemical baths over many months. First she casts the figures from live models and then begins the chemical peels. The erosion is layered and uneven and the figures seem to wither away. When they look like they've been weathered by centuries, she destroys them. To me they are inexpressibly sad. The narrative of humanity. I think she's a genius."

"But why does she feel compelled to destroy them? They become more and more disturbing and beautiful. I feel very strongly about their survival."

"I asked her the same question. All she could say was that she had to, as if this was necessary and inevitable. When I thought about it, it made complete sense to me.

"I proposed that we stage her figures. This is one in a series of figures of all shapes and sizes, both genders, in simple environments. I like the challenge of photographing them so that the sculptural integrity is honored, and the photo becomes a companion work of art."

"Very clever, because this way the work is preserved."

She looked very pleased that he got that.

"How did you meet her?"

"I met her in Vermont, this past spring. Remember? I was invited to an open house for artists at the Vermont Studio Center. My friend had a connection to the place and said I should come."

"Who was the friend?"

"You don't know her. She lives some of the year in Brooklyn and some in Vermont."

Howard felt an old, familiar pang of jealousy that was so much a part of his history with T.J., an embarrassing kneejerk reaction. It was ridiculous of course, particularly since he was seeing Solange.

He changed the subject. "Where's Sinclair?"

"Out."

"Out where?"

"Not sure."

T.J. walked past him out of the darkroom. He followed.

169

"What do you mean, not sure?" He could feel his temper rising.

As T.J. was walking up the stairs, he was trying to calm down. He had Glick in his head reminding him not to pick a fight. He took a breath and allowed himself to lag behind her so that he could compose himself.

When he walked into the kitchen, T.J. was pouring herself a glass of wine. She raised the bottle at him. "Want one?"

"Sure," he said, sitting down at the kitchen table. Maybe a glass of wine would help mellow him.

"Okay, so why didn't you ask her where she was going?"

"Because she was upset and I didn't want to pressure her."

This was going to be twenty questions.

T.J. put his glass of wine down in front of him and sat across from him at the farm table.

"Why was she upset?"

"Because she found out about you and Solange."

"How did she find out?"

"I told her."

"Why would you do that, T.J.?"

He kept his voice low and steady, even at great cost to himself. What would he do with his fury? How do you protect your child from the insensitivity of her own mother?

"I didn't think it would bother her that much. She accepts that I have affairs, but, curiously, she was really disturbed about your having one."

"She grew up with your affairs. She doesn't expect that behavior from me."

"That's what she said. I don't remember her exact words, but she implied that you were the dependable, moral one."

Was that it? Was this some kind of revenge because T.J. was upset about Solange? After all these years of T.J. urging him to make himself happy and be with other women and holding his inaction and suffering in contempt, now, when it happens, she's jealous? Or what? What does she feel about it?

"It's better that she knows."

"Why? Why is it better? Did you ever stop to consider how it would make her feel?"

"Surprised, of course, but I thought she'd take it in stride. We're not exactly a typical family."

"You're an idiot."

"What did you say?"

He didn't answer.

"Sorry. Forget I said that." He had to change his tone of voice. "T.J., I want you to tell me everything. What exactly did you tell her?"

"What difference does it make?"

T.J. was fidgeting. She looked like she would bolt from her chair at any moment.

"Actually, I asked Sinclair not to be here tonight. To stay with a friend. I wanted this time alone with you, to talk."

Howard had barely touched his wine. He wanted to have a sober conversation with T.J., realizing he really didn't want to be mellowed or blurred around the edges. He wanted to be alert; he needed to be. T.J., on the other hand, had already finished her first glass, got up to bring the bottle to the table, and poured herself another. This was T.J. distraught, or this was T.J. sad, angry, happy. T.J. drank. He never could really admit to himself how much, because she was high-functioning. Was she an alcoholic? He just thought of her as a drinker. Not as someone who couldn't stop.

"I'm not completely telling you everything I said to Sinclair."

Howard felt fear in the pit of his stomach.

"I want you to know I would never have told her. She goaded me into it."

"What do you mean she goaded you into it? What, are you a child?"

T.J. normally would have reacted. The fight would have been on, and the escalation would have led to her departure within a day or two. But she always came back. Sometimes he wished she wouldn't. But mostly he was relieved when she did. He told himself, for Sinclair's sake, but that was only a partial truth.

She ignored his remark.

"There's something I've never told you." And then, while she drank half the bottle of wine, she told him about her father.

Howard listened. For once, he knew better than to interrupt. It was another moment, among many in his life with T.J., when he realized he didn't know the woman he was married to. That she could keep something that significant to herself. He felt anger in all directions, but also a canyon of sympathy for T.J. and for his daughter. The burden of his wife's experience was a trauma all its own, and then the transference of this knowledge to his daughter, already reeling from the news of his infidelity... He felt like the world was splitting from an earthquake of betrayals.

He stood up and pulled T.J. to her feet. She stiffened in his arms and pushed her hands against his chest.

"T.J.," he said quietly. "I'm sorry."

She thrashed her head from side to side, but he didn't release her.

"I'm sorry, T.J."

She whimpered.

"I'm sorry, T. J."

She started sobbing so violently that she began to retch, and then her body convulsed and she threw up. His shirt was covered in her wine-thinned vomit. And he still held her. He kissed the top of her head, her body now limp in his arms.

"I'm sorry, Howard."

She was still weeping, but quietly. She wiped her mouth on her sleeve. He smelled the sick all over him. He didn't care. He would put her in the shower. He would take off his clothes and deal with them later. He would carry her to bed and kiss her on the forehead as she instantly fell asleep. Then he would take his own shower and cry.

T.J.

When T.J. woke up the next morning Howard was still beside her in bed. Sensing that she was awake, he rolled over toward her.

"You're awake," he said.

"I woke up just now. Have you been awake?"

"Oh, maybe for an hour or so."

She reached for his hand and interlaced her fingers in his. They used to do this, just lie in bed and watch their hands twined together, saying nothing.

"You know, I loved my father when I was really young. I was a daddy's girl."

He raised her hand in his and kissed a knuckle.

"My childhood had been like living in a glass house that suddenly, and finally, shattered," she continued. "I'm glad you stayed."

Did she mean in bed this morning, or all their years together?

"I feel like my skin has been peeled off, Howard. It's a feeling I don't like."

"It's scary, right?"

She looked at him, surprised. "Yes. How did you know?"

"Because I've felt like that, too."

She freed her hand and ran it down his cheek, regarding him. "I'm sorry Howard."

He never thought he'd hear these words from T.J. A part of him wanted to ask, 'sorry for what?' He felt greedy for more. But Glick had said, "Just listen."

She moved against his body, which confused him. Was he supposed to be the father or the lover? His body always welcomed T.J.'s After all this time, that hadn't changed. He put a tentative hand on T.J.'s breast. She didn't pull away. He thought of Solange.

SOLANGE

What was she thinking? She was looking at herself in the mirror above her dressing table. She was still beautiful, but she could see the differences in the contours of her face and knew how she looked today at fifty-seven compared to even five years ago. It didn't matter. It seemed she would remain that piece of un-plucked ripe fruit about to burst from its skin. She knew better than to have gotten involved with Howard. But he got to her because he wasn't slick. He didn't rush at her like a dog with hungry loins. He was endearingly open. She thought he was a grownup, and that maybe she had found a peer, but she stupidly ignored the Gordian knot of family. In the beginning, if she was honest with herself, she didn't want a deep attachment, or anything permanent. But he grew on her, revealing her own hunger that she'd been disconnected from and had discounted. She didn't need a man, she told herself. But having awakened what is lovely about intimacy and attachment, about being playful, having a man respect her, well, that was hard to give up.

She sighed at her reflection. He goes back to T.J. and Sinclair, while she returns to empty space with an opened heart that she has to shut down. Again. It was true what she told Howard. She'd rather have loved and lost, than not to have loved at all. But as she got older, the cost increased. And the odds of being willing to open up again got smaller. And the odds of finding someone she would even bother with: also slim. So was it selfish of her to keep it going with Howard until he said enough, or was it self-destructive? It actually hadn't gone on that long. Six, seven months? It would be smart to end now. Less painful. Once he became something she depended on, it would be so much worse to let it go.

She applied hydrating oil to her face and gently rubbed it all over. She wished she could live in Paris—oh, God, that feeling of relief she had when she was there. She became completely herself. She was a human being named Solange. Not a black person, not lesser than. Not different from anyone else, except in the way that everyone is different from everyone else. It was a revelation. She fell in love with the whole city. She moved through the streets of Paris experiencing a delicious freedom: a sense of safety. She had cried all the way back on the plane, because she was leaving 'home.' Where she belonged. But there was no staying. The France gig was up, the band left before she did. She stole an extra few days just to be by herself. She had a teenage son and a troubled marriage waiting for her in the States.

As soon as she'd walked in the door, her stomach tensed. There it was, back in a New York minute: the same old, same old. Her husband sat on the couch drinking a beer, while her son played a video game. First words out of her mouth, "Charles, why aren't you doing your homework?" She couldn't help it. She couldn't run screaming from the apartment, so she said what she said.

"I missed you too, Mom," he replied, his resentment already filling the room.

"Clay," she nodded.

Her husband was looking at her. "Looks like Paris agreed with you."

She knew she shouldn't have spent the money and bought the coat, but it was Paris! A Parisian swing coat in pale yellow, with a deep shawl collar. She felt oh so very chic in it. And she got a deal. It wasn't new.

Ignoring her husband, she said, "I'm sorry, son. I'm glad to see you. I shouldn't have said that. How have you been?"

She took off her coat, hung it in the hall closet, left her suitcase on the floor, walked over to the couch and sat down next to Charles.

"I've been okay. How was the trip?"

He didn't look at her; he was too busy playing his game.

She began telling them both how wonderful it was, but neither of them was listening. Her heart was beating heavily in her chest and for a moment she felt like she couldn't breathe.

"You okay, Solange?

She glanced at Clay. Handsome Clay. After everything he'd put her through, she could still think that.

"Just fatigue and jetlag. I'm fine."

She daubed white dots of cream under her eyes and patted gently. She looked at herself skeptically. "I'm fine."

Another memory. Coming out of a movie with Howard, and apropos of nothing, Howard started singing to her.

"She's so fine...Yeah, yeah...Gotta make her mine...come on Solange, sing it with me."

"It's, 'HE's so fine,' Howard."

"I don't care. C'mon. SHE's so fine..."

"You want me to be the girl backup-singer, to do the 'Yeah, yeah's?"

"Yes, I do."

He began walking backwards and snapping his fingers. She laughed because he was making these silly sixties dance moves and repeating, "She's so fine..." then pausing, waiting for her.

"Yeah, yeah," she sang.

He grinned, nodding his head.

"Gotta make her mine."

"Yeah, yeah."

"Sooner or later."

"Yeah, yeah."

"I hope it's not later."

They were dancing on the sidewalk. She shimmied her shoulders forward at him and he shimmied back. They were making a spectacle of themselves. Who does this in their fifties, in public? They did.

Then he stepped beside her and sang softly, leaning toward her, "'I just can't wait! I just can't wait! To be held in her arms.'"

She couldn't help but smile, remembering.

That husband of hers, Clay, wasn't like that. When she first met him and was getting to know him, she'd asked, "Do you ever smile?"

"No," he said.

"Why not?"

"Because when I was a kid, I smiled all the time. The boys in school would make fun of me, treated me like I was an idiot. Then after school they beat me up. They taunted, 'Smile, Clay. Let's see you smile.'

So, I stopped. I promised myself I would only smile if I wanted to, not because it was expected."

And then, he smiled at her. It was like he'd just given her a present.

This is what men do. This is how they enter your heart. How could you not love them when they can be delicious, like powdered sugar, sweetening your life?

Why can't it stay like that? Instead of all the sad and unnecessary losses that seem so very necessary and urgent at the time.

Clay got up from the couch, walked over to her suitcase, and picked it up.

"What are you doing, Clay?"

"I'm carrying your suitcase into the bedroom for you."

He said it like it was the most natural thing in the world, like this is what he always did for her. He paused, standing behind her while she sat on the couch, and touched her shoulder. He bent over, and whispered, so Charles wouldn't hear him. Not that Charles would have. He was lost in his video world of "Doom."

Now what? She had just gotten home. She was exhausted.

"Goodnight, Charles." She leaned over and kissed her son's cheek.

"Night, mom." Not even a sideways glance, not a flicker of emotion.

Solange sat down on the side of the bed while Clay stood. It was her bedroom. He wouldn't be there if he hadn't said, "We have to talk."

"While you were gone, Charles and I spoke about his coming to live with me in California after he graduates."

"Wow, you bonded with Charles that quickly? I was gone three weeks and he wants to live with you?"

"Well, bonding was the point, wasn't it, Solange?"

"Babysitting was the point. I didn't want my teenage son to be alone for three weeks, and he couldn't just leave school and go to you, could he?"

"I think this will be a good change for him. I want this. He wants this. Really, it's his decision to make."

Her son's decision. Clay's decision. Howard's decision. She turned away from herself in the mirror, depressed. She didn't usually indulge in self-pity. She was better than that. But it was being triggered by the situation with Howard, and she was angry. How did she manage to love men who couldn't love her back? Not permanently. Like she wasn't enough, when she knew she was more than enough. She deserved better. Married a preacher who discovered he didn't believe in God and the hypocrisy was eating him alive. He felt so much shame. Then he cheated on her. He drank. He gambled. The only addiction he didn't have was drugs. Charles was five when Clay left to find another life and identity. He just couldn't tell his congregation. He didn't have the courage. But even that was bullshit. He left because he fell in love with another woman. He left Solange his debts and he left his son to be raised alone as he disappeared into his "search for himself." Strong black woman rises to the occasion, and hell, yes, she did. Her son was a good man, even if he had to go through being a fucked-up teenager. He turned out okay. Clay became a community organizer and political activist. Even he turned out okay.

She'd married him because he had the charisma of Jesus, and was as handsome as the devil. He was a solid citizen. They could have a stable life and she could be the artist she wanted to be. He would preach and have his own church and she would sing in the choir on Sundays, and in jazz clubs all the rest of the week. She thought they were a match made in heaven. Amen.

Ah, men. She nodded her head at her own foolishness. Which, if she really thought about it, was just random luck, her bad luck. Because, what had she done—or believed differently from a million other women? Everyone marries believing it will last 'til death do you part. And Howard. Who'd have thunk it? In middle-age she'd become smitten with a white, Jewish, married musician from Brooklyn. A liberal, nonbeliever. A man whose need reached inside and spoke to her own. And he adored her. Not the words. Not only the words— he played, and nuzzled, and fucked her so that she felt herself all the way down to her bones. He made love to her like Paris. She became Solange in Paris when she was with him. The mystery was, she didn't know why. She knew one thing. She didn't want to emotionally take care of another man to help him through his crisis, a crisis that had nothing to do with her, but which ended in her loss.

* * *

I want to stay with Solange.

I'm very sorry, Howard, but you can't.

Why?

Because that's not how the story goes.

But you're making it up.

I am.

But you could change it. I'm asking.

I wish I could Howard.

I could be happy with Solange. I could have a different life.

Howard, the story is the story.

Well, what if an editor wanted you to change it?

I would definitely think about changing it.

Well?

You're not the editor. You're the character.

I'm the prisoner, the slave, the...

I've never had what you want.

But this is fiction. You can change it!

I can't make stuff up that isn't true to my own experience.

Do you know anybody in a successful long-term relationship? The kind that only ends when death they do part.

Yes, a few.

Well, then. You could write about that.

I can't, because I don't know how they work.

Truly?

Truly. I can't imagine my way into them.

I want to talk to Dr. Glick.

Right now?

Yes.

DR. GLICK

"I know I haven't seen you in a while. Thank you for taking me on such short notice."

Glick was leaning forward in his chair, legs crossed, elbows on the armrests, his fingers laced, looking at Howard.

"I want to stay with Solange."

"So why don't you?"

"I can't."

"Why not?"

"I can't explain it. It's like it's not in my control."

Glick leaned back in his chair pondering, his chin now resting on his hand.

There was a silence while they were both thinking.

"What happened?"

"T. J. happened."

"What does that mean?"

"You were right. She wants to keep me."

"How do you know this?"

"She basically thanked me for not leaving her."

"Okay."

"She said she was sorry, to me. She's never apologized before. But that's not it. I mean, those things matter. It matters that she's treating me differently, better, like what I've been wanting for a long time. We've even had sex."

Glick's eyebrows shot up in surprise.

"But, I've fallen in love with Solange. I see a different life with her. She's a warm, loving, person. She really wants to have sex with me." He groaned. "God, it's been so long...I'd forgotten what that feels like. But, I feel guilty all the time. I feel like I betray each one with the other... And then there's Sinclair."

He looked at Glick. "She knows."

"Ahhh."

"Yes. T.J. told her. See what I mean?"

"Yes," Glick said. "How does that make you feel?"

"Enraged. Punished. But, here's where it gets complicated. I feel touched."

"Touched? Why?"

"Because it means she's that desperate."

"Not punitive?"

'Yes, that too. But it means she's scared, and she would only be scared if I mattered."

"How do you know it's not a power struggle? Her ego, her vanity won't let you go."

"I don't know. That's the thing. I don't know."

"What happens if you stay?"

186

"Then maybe I'm a sucker."

"Or, maybe you begin to have the family you want."

"God, you are not making this easier."

Glick smiled. "What do you want, Howard?"

"I want to be with Solange. I want Sinclair to not care that I am, just like she didn't care about Cherie or all the others T.J. was with."

"Could you do that to Solange? Would she tolerate it?"

"She is now. She knew about the wife and daughter when we got involved."

"But things changed."

"Yes, things changed."

"Always the risk."

"Worth the risk. That's what she would say."

"Do you still love T.J.?"

He stopped and thought. Then, he tried to get out of his head to just find the feeling. Instead he found an image of putting her in the shower and washing the vomit off her. Of putting her to bed. Of her taking his hand and lacing her fingers into his. Each image made his heart throb. What was the word for that? Was that love?

SINCLAIR

The night she was banished from the house by T.J. was not spent at her friend's house. She was too freaked out to see even her closest friend. She didn't want to talk about it. Not to anyone. She wanted to seethe. She wanted to hold onto her anger because it kept her from feeling afraid. She rode into the city and walked. Her hands were fisted at her sides and she almost wished someone would try and start something with her, because she would come down on them like a rain of ter-ror—she liked her pun—a cloud-burst of rage, bewildering and soaking her would-be attackers in their own blood. Her brain pinged between these self-conscious thoughts, then ponged into a state of such internal distraction that she didn't know what she'd been thinking. When her eyes focused on where she was it was like coming awake in the middle of a dream.

She was on 14th street in Manhattan and a wig store

caught her eye. She ducked in and started looking around. This felt right. This was what she needed. She needed a wig. Her hair was short now so she wanted something longer, maybe a bob, or even shoulder length. Her own hair color was reddish brown, so she thought she'd go either blonde or dark brunette. A sales woman was skulking around, and when she looked like she was on the verge of approaching, T.J. would walk further away, trying to discourage her. But then she picked up a black, chin-length wig, and put it on. She gave it a tug to fit it in place and realized that wearing a wig would be hot, and she didn't mean, "hot," as in, "she's so..."

"Makes you look older," the saleswoman said as Sinclair was looking at herself in the mirror.

"It's a look I'm going for. For this surprise party."

"I think," the saleswoman said, evaluating her face, "you'd look better as a blonde. You have fair skin. Unless, of course, you want to look like a vampire that hasn't fed in awhile."

That made her laugh. Sinclair liked her. More importantly, she liked the distraction of the conversation. At another time she would have been really annoyed that this woman had the presumption to offer an opinion. Maybe she wanted to look anemic. It was none of her business. But right now, it was a manageable human connection that allowed her to focus outside herself. She even felt grateful.

Sinclair followed her to the blonde wigs and put her hands on one with big hair and long blonde curls. Something Dolly Parton would wear. She actually wanted to try it on. Just to see. Just for fun, but the saleswoman had picked up a rather chic, shiny synthetic, shoulder-length wig of straight hair and thick bangs. It was like a sci-fi wig a beautiful female robot would wear.

The saleswoman gave it a shake and handed it to her.

Looking at her reflection in the mirror, she felt like someone she didn't know. She liked it.

"That looks perfect on you. Very becoming. It sets off your pretty eyes."

She did like the way the bangs covered her eyebrows, framing her father's blue eyes and double row of long lashes. A rare genetic feature. Elizabeth Taylor, she'd learned, had it. Made her eyes, and Howard's eyes, look like they were wearing mascara. She actually favored T.J.'s features but she got Howard's eyes. He said they both inherited this from his mother. For a forlorn moment, she wished she had grandparents. Weren't they the ones that spoiled you? Didn't it help to have other people love you because you were related?

"How much?" T.J. asked, taking it off her head.

"Thirty dollars."

T.J. slipped her backpack off her shoulder and fished around inside for her wallet. She handed the saleswoman her debit card. She could spend up to a monthly limit that her mother transferred to her account. The account was not in T.J.'s name, however, and Sinclair had insisted that her mother couldn't monitor it. If Sinclair over-spent, she wasn't to come crying to Mommy for more money; but, other than that, she could do what she wanted. It was her money to waste, spend, or save. Thirty was more than she wanted to pay, but fuck it.

Before leaving the store, she put the wig on. She felt different. She actually smiled. True, it was sarcastic and bitter, as smiles went, but it was an improvement over the scowl she wore tromping down the street with her hands balled. She wasn't making fists now. She was occupied by what to call herself. She needed a new name. Dusty, Mickee, Misha, Dakota... She couldn't decide.

She felt her backpack being tugged off her body from behind, pulling her backwards.

"GET THE FUCK AWAY FROM ME!" arose deep and demonic from the very bottom of her belly.

She sounded terrifying. She turned, still clinging to the backpack with one arm and saw a teenage boy hightailing it away from her. She gulped in air, bent over, her hands on her knees, utterly shaken both by the assault and this self-protective thing she had become. Who was that? Who was she? She'd always thought that if anyone ever tried to rob her she would just give it up. Nothing was worth getting hurt or dying over. *Hey man, take my money, here.* But now, when push came to shove, she realized it wasn't in her control. She would have killed to save her stuff. It made no sense, completely irrational. But she was also impressed with herself. Another Sinclair had put in an appearance. A dude you don't fuck with. Still shaky, and proud, she stood upright and descended into the subway. She wanted escape, to calm down, she felt too hopped up. She headed downtown to The Film Forum to see what was playing.

She escaped into *Crouching Tiger, Hidden Dragon*. She was able to stop thinking for the duration. The sword fight in the treetops took her breath away. The mood still lingered; she felt warrior-like when she walked out.

What time was it? It was dark.

She was almost eighteen, it was 2002, and she still wasn't

allowed to have a cell phone. Howard didn't believe in them, as though their existence depended on belief, like God, and T.J. disdained them. When she argued that she could be reached if she had one and they wouldn't have to worry about where she was, they rolled their eyes at her. They weren't buying it. Emergencies? Use a pay phone. Or use a friend's phone, was their answer. It's not like they couldn't afford it. They were just old. They didn't get it.

"Excuse me," she said to a woman coming out of the theater. "Do you have the time?"

"Sure," the woman said, reaching into her pocket and pulling out her flip phone and checking.

"It's 8:05."

Wow, she realized the movie was over two hours long.

"Did you just see *Crouching Tiger, Hidden Dragon*?" the woman asked.

"Yes."

"Weren't the visuals stunning?"

"Amazing."

"Hey, are you alone? Do you want to get coffee and talk about it? I'm dying to talk about it. Or, a drink?"

"Um..."

"If you've got somewhere you need to be..."

She looked at this woman. She looked to be in her twenties. Shaggy brunette hair, shorter than Sinclair, a gap-toothed smile, and no makeup. She looked harmless. And nice. Why not? Another adventure in the life of Sinclair. It's not like her parents were wondering about where she was. *Please, don't come home tonight.* There was the twist again in her stomach.

"Sure," she said.

"I'm Nina," the woman said, sticking out her hand to shake. "What's your name?"

"Dakota." She smiled back at the happy face of the stranger standing in front of her, quickly shaking her hand.

So, that was the name of her blonde, alien self: Dakota.

"Dakota. Nice. That's not a name you hear coming and going."

"My father liked the movie *Badlands*."

"I like *Badlands*. Another visually beautiful film."

They were walking now. She let Nina lead.

"Where are we going?" Sinclair had the presence of mind to ask.

"Um. Let me think. Well, my place is walking distance. I have wine. I have pot. But, no, no. That would be crazy, right?" She laughed.

Sinclair tensed up. "Well..."

"Yeah, no, bad idea. It's just that I feel like I know you."

"You do?"

"Yeah. You feel familiar to me."

Dakota grinned. "Must be my hair."

"Your hair is fabulous. How do you get it so shiny?"

"Great drugstore shampoo." It probably looked better at night, she thought. Not so fake.

"How about we go to Henrietta Hudson. It's about two minutes from here. Ever been?"

"No, but I'm game."

"I like a gal who's game." They were walking side-by-side and Nina was about a half-foot shorter than she was. She could see her lighter roots.

They chatted about the movie and discussed how the special effects may have been done for the flying sword scene, and the whole time Sinclair felt less aware of the knot in her stomach. But there was also a new kind of fear, mixed with excitement, from not knowing what Dakota was capable of.

* * *

You could have at least given her a fucking cellphone.

YOU could have given her a cellphone, Howard.

I will now. Go back and write it into a scene.

Nope, too late.

Are you sure you got that right? Didn't everybody have a cellphone in 2000?

Many T.J.'s age certainly did. You, maybe not. Not your generation. But, eventually, everyone was brought to their knees by smartphones. I think five-year-olds have them now. Hell, they master them at one. But people like you and T.J. were certainly hold-outs. For the two of you, it would have been out of the question to give an eighteen-year-old their own phone. Might have when she went away to college.

Are you older than me?

Younger.

Would I find you attractive?

Drop dead gorgeous.

With or without the wig?

With. My hair is thinning.

You're always fucking with me.

It's my job.

* * *

And then they were there, and Nina was opening the door to HH Bar and Girl. Inside it was warm and lively;, the bartender was pouring drinks into a row of glasses and, the D.J. was spinning Pink's "Most Girls."

She relaxed. Better than that, her spirit lifted. They found a cushioned, corner spot. Several people smiled and mouthed, "Hi," at Nina.

"You're a regular?"

"My neighborhood bar," she answered. "Waddya want to drink?"

"Oh, I'll just have a beer."

"Drinks on me. Have something more festive."

Festive. She liked that word. Nobody she knew said 'festive.'

Dakota, entirely poised, said, "Surprise me."

"That's my girl."

She stood up and went to the bar to order. Sinclair watched the animated conversation with the bartender and then her eyes drifted across the room. Women were dancing. The guys here looked gay, although there were some straight looking couples. Tourists. Like her. And the women were very attractive. Mostly women, talking, flirting, and dancing together. And then it dawned on her. Lesbian bar. She was slow on the uptake. But how could she know? Lack of experience. That meant that Nina was hitting on her. But she kind of already thought that maybe that was happening. It would also make it less threatening. Not a psycho. Just gay. Like her mom. Maybe like her, even. She had no idea, really. She was equally attracted to men and women. But she didn't actually like men. She liked women. Dakota was gay. She decided it right then. Sinclair? Not entirely sure. But Dakota was definitely gay.

"I ordered us both Cosmopolitans."

The pink girlie drink from *Sex and the City*. And now she'd get to taste one. She took a sip. Wow, it tasted amazing. She sipped again.

"Good?"

Dakota smiled, suddenly very happy, but not from the drink—which was certainly part of the adventure, but from all of it. The escape she'd created into another reality today was saving her.

Nina took a sip herself. "They make great Cosmos here. Best bartender in town, and a cutie."

"I didn't know we were going to a gay bar," she admitted.

"Do you mind?"

"Not at all."

Another pleased smile from Nina.

"You are, you know."

"What?"

"Gay. That's why I said I knew you, that you were familiar."

Gooseflesh creeped up the backs of Sinclair's arms. How could this woman see what she didn't even know about herself? Was it the fruit of the womb—T.J.s womb—that had a scent of its own? What did Nina see that made her so certain?

"Relax, Dakota. Your secret's safe with me. No one else knows but me, and this entire bar full of lesbians." She laughed and raised her glass to her lips. "Come on, enjoy the drink, this moment, and me. I hope you're enjoying me."

She didn't mince words did she? What a bold-assed woman. This thought heated her along with the alcohol from the drink, which was very good. She admired bold. She wanted to be bold. She took another swallow of the drink.

"Wanna dance?" Dakota asked.

"Now you're talking my language."

Nina had on skintight jeans. She had a bubble butt. Very cute. She was also wearing red suede high-heeled shoes that Sinclair hadn't even noticed before. That was a little scary, how oblivious she was because of her self-absorption. What else didn't she see?

It also meant that Nina was even shorter than Sinclair thought. Maybe even three inches shorter. When Sinclair was younger, her father would measure her against the doorframe with a yardstick and a pencil, writing the dates, and he'd say, "Why, you're so short I can eat a bowl of soup off the top of your head." She thought it was silly and funny. That was her dad. She felt tears welling up and she knew she was going to start to cry. She left the dance floor with Nina on it, grabbed her backpack from their seats and went in search of the ladies' room. Thank God it was empty. She closed the door and burst into tears. In a few minutes, she heard a knock.

"Are you okay, Dakota?"

"Yes," she managed.

She threw some cold water on her face and dried her eyes with paper towels, looked at her ridiculously wonderful wig and then opened the door and let Nina in.

Nina took one look at her and closed the space between them, presumptuously putting her arms around her, which felt like a child was hugging her, which she thought was funny. So funny that she burst into tears again while keeping her arms at her sides. But Nina didn't let go, and then she slowly hugged Nina back.

SOLANGE

Howard gave her a sad smile when he showed up at her door. Uh-oh.

He had picked up Chinese food on his way and handed the bag to her. For some reason that annoyed her. It was her apartment after all, but it felt like a hand off that men make to women unconsciously—here, you take care of the food. You're the woman. Such a small, meaningless gesture on his part—and this was probably just her resentment poking through—but, she had to admit, there was even a small sting about his acting like the white master. Whoa, this was crazy thinking. All the man did, Solange, was hand you a bag of Chinese food that he generously picked up. What your feeling? This is not about him. This is about you.

She went into the kitchen and opened the bag on the counter, got out some plates and silverware, and spooned out General Tso's Chicken and vegetable lo mein. She could feel him waiting for her to ask, 'What's wrong, Howard?' but she wasn't going to ask. This was her night, and she wanted Howard the smitten, Howard the lover. She wanted the play and compliments. She wanted him to come up behind her and kiss her neck while she was busy with the food. She wanted him to say that she smelled delicious and she would say, 'That's the chicken you're smelling.' He would put his arms around her from behind and whisper, 'I love chicken.' Because that's who they were together, and that's what she wanted tonight. She sighed, put the food on the table, and sat down.

"I'm not going to do this, Howard."

"You're not going to do what?"

"I'm not going to be the mistress that you come to, to be emotionally taken care of."

She saw his look of annoyance. "I didn't ask you for anything."

"Yes, you did. And it's not fair."

"When? When did I ask you?"

"The moment you came through the door."

She could see that he got it, but there was something petulant in his expression and she knew he didn't want to know. There it was, the resistance, the lack of understanding about the position he was putting her in. No apology. Then he played his trump card.

"T.J. told Sinclair about us."

She saw him visibly sag when he said this. She didn't want to see this. And there it was. The other shoe had dropped. Even though she'd been waiting for this moment to happen, there was no way to prepare. It was the difference between knowing someone is dying and what it feels like when they're dead. Hadn't she been the one to say their relationship was on life support?

She touched his arm and he looked at her with a hopefulness that made her tender. Damn men. Her sympathy for him and the hurt that Sinclair must be feeling made her feel guilty. Then defensive. She wasn't the one who was married. It was his burden, not hers. And yet, she felt it anyway. She cared less about T.J. Hadn't she been pushing this for years? How perverse that woman was.

"I'm worried about my daughter. She doesn't want to speak to me. The only thing she's said is, 'When are you moving out?'"

"What did you say?"

"I told her I wasn't."

This stabbed her heart. He had said, more than once, that Sinclair was the most important love of his life, that losing her would not be in the same galaxy of pain that losing T.J. or Solange would be. She thought bitterly, *love is a many-splintered thing.*

"What do you want to do, Howard?"

"I don't want to lose my daughter. I don't want to lose you."

And T.J., she added in her own thoughts. *You don't want to lose T.J.* Wasn't this classic? Wasn't this cliché? And human—the mess from craving validation and love. You could go on a starvation diet for just so long and then you had to eat cake.

* * *

I feel terrible about Solange.

Good. You should, Howard.

Good? This must be about you then. Okay... Who was he?

Not important.

Did he leave his wife?

I didn't ask him to.

Did you want him to?

Part of me did.

And the other part?

Feared the fantasy future would just fall apart.

Fifty-fifty chance?

Something like that.

Do you still see him?

No.

Talk to him?

Sometimes.

Do you still love him?

Yes.

How do you cope?

I wrote a message, put it in a bottle, and sent it out to sea.

And now?

And now, I live on my desert island.

T.J.

It was a horrible thing to admit, but after she told Sinclair and Howard, she felt a relief she hadn't anticipated. She'd never wanted to tell anyone about her father, and then the surprise of family, the pressure of it, the demand that other people make on you, turned out to be a gift. She had never truly understood this; that what was emotionally complicated, and therefore burdensome to you, was something that could save you. That did save you. She felt an utterly unexpected softening toward Howard, like an echo from the old days when she still felt a call and response. She could never understand her own reactions. She just lived on what drove her, in her art, in her love life. She never refused her need, whatever the consequences, because she was more committed to herself than to anyone else. Did that make her selfish and immoral? She didn't know. She felt like she couldn't be the judge.

But her daughter; she had truly unfathomable feelings about Sinclair. She was afraid of her own daughter. It had nothing to do with who Sinclair actually was. It had to do with a fear of contaminating her, of failing her, and the irony was that she had, and did. Sinclair was of her body and was too close. She was afraid of that attachment and need. It created such heartache in her that she fled. She didn't analyze, she just acted. Re-acted. Re-enacted. She didn't want to know. She didn't want this. And yet, she loved Sinclair, from a distance, like a twin she had been separated from.

Now that she wasn't seeing anyone else, and things had calmed down, she was with Howard. She never projected onto the future, so she didn't think about how long this would last. But she had one constant in her life—her art. And to her astonishment, she was in bloom. She was fertile, a garden of ideas, and she was doing her best work.

She was working on a new show that she thought might sustain her interest for a few years as variations on a theme. She had been reading a magazine article on Chinese foot binding which contained appalling images showing the process of breaking and wrapping a young girl's feet to produce the idealized three inch foot. On the same page was an advertisement for very expensive stiletto-heeled shoes, with the model's foot contorted into a brutally unnatural position—both the article and advertising images promoted sexualized foot fashions. She must have unconsciously been mulling this over because she had awakened in the middle of the night, found her notebook and starting writing furiously, unable to keep up with the images in her head.

This was her real life. This was what sustained her.

NOTES: A visual encyclopedia of the bizarre female standards of beauty from around the world, some from other centuries.

The name of the collection: "Complicity"

1) Start doing "fashion" shoots in black and white. Very stark.

2) Incorporate existing shots of women from around the world with the staged photos. Some would become photomontages. Some would be juxtaposed next to each other, or displayed in a series.

KOREA

Head shot of a nineteen-year-old Korean woman. Very normal, naturally pretty.

1) Same woman is shown in a series of companion images of her nose surgery, her jaw surgery, her double lid surgery, and injections to reshape her cheeks and forehead.

2) The final beauty shot shows the barely recognizable, "improved" woman. Have text call-outs imposed on the image listing the twenty-two products used to give her a flawless, "natural" complexion and big eyes.

USA

1) Fashion shot of a woman from the neck down with huge breasts leaning forward, the breasts spilling out of the dress. Maybe this is the shot at the center, and there is a surrounding photo montage of breasts being evaluated for enhancement surgery. Before and Afters. A shot of what the actual surgery looks like.

2) Erotic/porn shot of a woman lying on her back with

her legs spread showing her perfect, Brazilian-waxed, little vagina.

3) Montage of normal women's vaginas.

4) Separate shots of before and after reconstructive surgery for labia, mons, clitoral hood reduction, etc.

Her list grew: China, Brazil, India, Burma, Nigeria, Ethiopia, Indonesia, Kenya, Etc.

OBSERVATION: Consistent to all the beauty "enhancements" was that pain was involved. Meeting male expectations of beauty meant enduring physical pain—pain that was either forced on you, or that was endured willingly. Another form of complicity.

Questions/speculations for research:

Where does this come from? What are the impulses of fashion and fetishism? Continuums on the same spectrum? If women conform they have a kind of power—their desirability—and if that's their only power then how satisfied are the women, how successful do they feel? How many feel at its mercy? Reduced. When women accept the beauty standards, are they happier because it gives them status? If men become powerless at the sight of a small, slippered foot, wanting to prostrate themselves and kiss the tiny toe, then who has the power and who is giving it up? Cost/benefit?

So much to research. She would have to travel, of course. She'd have to apply for grants, get the funding she needed. Howard simply couldn't leave her. He had to be here for Sinclair. Really, what was she worrying about? She already knew the answer. Howard wasn't going anywhere.

HOWARD

He knocked on Sinclair's bedroom door. She'd been avoiding him for weeks—either not home, or asleep. He told T.J. he'd be coming in late; T.J. was at an opening, so Sinclair thought she'd be home alone.

"Sinclair?" He paused. "I'm coming in." He sounded like the police.

She was siting up in bed, her headphones around her neck. She'd heard him.

Sullen teenage daughter, wearing T.J.'s frown. It was crappy how children unconsciously mimicked their parent's expressions and mannerisms. Bad enough to look in the mirror, to see yourself looking more and more like your mother—your aged mother.

He approached the bed. "Sinclair, we have to talk." He pulled the desk chair up to the side of the bed.

"No, we don't. It doesn't matter. You can move out."

"See? This is why I want to talk, because who says I'm moving out? And it does matter."

"No, it doesn't. I have a girlfriend. I can move in with her." Arms crossed, slumping.

"What?!"

"Yeah, she has an apartment in the city."

T.J.'s cocky half smile.

He wanted to wipe that expression off Sinclair's face. Calm the shit down, Howard. Don't take the bait.

"Do you mind telling me what you're talking about?"

"Why should I tell you anything? You hide things. In fact, everyone in this family hides things." She looked at him. "Especially me."

What the fuck did that mean? More provocation. A smack of fear. His fear.

"Okay, okay. You're right. We all lie. Either to protect ourselves, or the people we love."

She snorted. "Great family values, Dad."

'Dad' was horribly sarcastic. More smirking. He hated teenagers. He was sure his face was flushed. Maybe he would just have a heart attack and die on the spot. Then she'd be sorry. Yeah, he was the mature one.

"Did you lie to Solange? Not that I care."

"No."

"Just to us?"

"T.J. knew."

"Then, just me."

He felt like he'd just put a stake through her heart.

"I was trying to protect you." That sounded so lame.

"Look, I'm sorry about the fact that I fell in love with Solange. I didn't plan to. I never wanted you to feel threatened."

"When were you going to tell me? When you were packing your bags?"

"I didn't say anything because I didn't really know what I was doing."

"But you love her?"

"Yes."

"And what about Mom?"

Sinclair was picking aggressively at a thread on her blanket, unraveling it, making a hole. He wanted to tell her to stop. It was driving him nuts.

"I love her, too, and before you even have to ask, I love you. Actually, Sinclair, I love you above all else. That's a lot of why I can't leave. I could never leave you."

He thought he saw a flicker of pain.

"I know you and Mom have a really fucked up marriage, but I just thought you both wanted it the way it was. Otherwise, you'd get divorced."

"It's just not that easy to understand."

"Now you're going to tell me I'm too young to understand." Her contempt from her wound, dripping blood.

"Did I say that?"

"I've always wondered why you and Mom stay together. It's a question I've asked myself since I was old enough to understand anything about the two of you, and that was pretty young."

Now it was a stake through his heart. Not only couldn't he protect her from strangers in the world, he couldn't protect her from himself.

"It's a good question, Rosie," he said, his sadness palpable now. Her angry expression deflated, her hand stilled.

"Look, it's not like you fall in love with the same person you end up being married to. Everyone changes, and at each point along the way, you choose to continue, to love, or to leave. It's a negotiation, not just with someone else's heart, but also with your own."

He had no idea how much of this meant anything to her.

"But there are happy couples, right? You and Mom are sometimes happy?" She glanced at him, hopefully—*say yes, please say yes.*

"Yes, Rosie, yes. And every couple is different. There's no right or wrong way. It's just what works for the two people. Sometimes what works is being miserable together. I know that sounds weird. But it doesn't have to be like that. Sometimes it's terrific."

"Can it stay terrific?" she asked, her eyes lingering on his face.

'Yes, it can. T.J. and I are not what you're doomed to. You will have something better. I know it."

He was thinking of Solange. He was thinking that he couldn't have even said this before her. She restored belief in him. But how do you even begin to explain to a seventeen-year-old what you're still figuring out in your fifties?

"I already do know." Sinclair smiled, a genuine happy face.

Wow. "Your girlfriend?"

God, he didn't want to know. He liked that family members had secrets.

"That's great. Really great," he continued. "Do you want to tell me about her?"

"I do want to, but..."

"But what?"

"Well, it's a really good thing, a great thing for me, but I'm not sure you'll be happy about it."

"Well, let's start with I'm surprised it's a girl, but I'm not exactly shocked."

"Do you mind?" She peered up at him. She looked so achingly young. Couldn't they just stop talking and hug?

"No."

"Are you disappointed?"

"No." He realized that he really didn't care. He was more concerned with who this person was.

"Would I like her?" he asked.

"Does that matter?" Dukes raised again. "Isn't it just important that I love her?"

"Your loving her may not be the most reliable way of my knowing who she is. If you have to think about her from your father's perspective, I might learn a lot more."

She considered this. "Wow. That's really kind of smart of you, Dad."

That made him smile.

Another pause. "I really don't know if you'll like her. I mean, you never liked any of Mom's girlfriends."

Smile gone. "That was different."

"You hated Cherie, and she was great."

Now he really tensed up.

"It's not the same. C'mon, you know it's not the same."

"I know it's different, but it's still about someone outside us."

He looked at her and thought, that was a brilliant thing to

say. That impressed him. How did she know all this at seven-teen? At seventeen he was a clueless dunce. He flashed on in-fant Rosie in his arms. How do you watch your child grow into an adult and then leave you? Because in fact, it was Sinclair who would be doing the leaving.

"Before we talk about your girlfriend, I just want to say one more thing. I know T.J. told you about her father. I hadn't known either. You want to talk about it?"

"No. I already talked about it with Nina."

That stung. He wanted her to talk with him. To want to. What kind of advice could another teenager give her? Wait a minute—she has her own apartment in Manhattan. How old is this girlfriend?

"Okay, I guess we talk about your girlfriend, Nina."

* * *

After they left the bar, they went to Nina's apartment, a studio with floor-to-ceiling bookshelves. Sinclair was a reader, but this was intimidating.

"You read all these?"

"Yes."

"Do you write?"

"No, but I teach. I'm a high school English teacher."

Oh, God, she doesn't know how old I am.

"Can I get you a beer?"

"Sure."

As Nina walked to the refrigerator, Sinclair was reading the book titles. About half the books were fiction, half were poetry. One caught her eye, and she pulled it from the shelf.

"What are you looking at?"

"*Group Portrait From Hell.*"

"Do you know it?"

"No, but I like the title." She put the volume back as Nina handed her a bottle of chilled pale ale.

"Pick a seat." She gestured grandly around the room, and laughed.

There was only one place to sit. Nina plopped down on the velvet burgundy couch.

"It also converts to my bed."

Sinclair sat down near her. She looked around for somewhere to put down her beer.

"Just put it on the floor. As you can see I'm a minimalist. I like uncluttered space. Table for eating, couch for sitting and sleeping, a lamp, and books, iPod for music."

Sinclair thought about what a pack rat she herself was, and a slob.

"Nice," she smiled. "All anyone really needs."

Nina's arm rested along the back of the couch. She reached out and touched Dakota's hair. Surprised, she quickly withdrew her hand. "Is that a wig?"

"Yes. Do you like it?" Dakota poofed up the sides of her fake blonde hair with her hands while pursing her lips into a moue.

"Take it off."

Dakota said, coyly, "What if I don't want to?"

"Dakota, please. I want to see what you really look like."

That made her nervous. What if she doesn't like my real hair? She reached up and very slowly tugged it from her head as Nina watched, making it feel erotic, like a strip tease.

"Okay, put it back on."

"What?" It was Sinclair's turn to be surprised. And upset.

Nina laughed at her. "I'm just kidding." She reached for Sinclair's real hair. "It's nice." She smoothed the hair, which was full of static electricity from the wig. Sinclair thought she probably looked ridiculous with the short strands sticking up all over.

"I think it suits you."

"You liked the wigged me better," Sinclair said, watching her expression.

"No, actually I like the natural you better, Dakota."

She blushed. "My name isn't Dakota."

Nina's smile disappeared.

"What?"

Nina was scrutinizing her, trying to take her measure. What was she thinking? "Just tell me your name."

"Sinclair."

"Are you making that up?"

"No, that's really my name."

Nina smiled. "That's even better than Dakota."

"You think?" She relaxed a little.

"Is there anything else I should know, Sinclair?"

Tension back. "My age?"

"Oh, God." Nina leaned away from her, her hands retreating to her lap. "How old are you?"

"I'll be eighteen in three months."

"You're in high school?!"

"Yes. But that's what makes it perfect. You're a high school teacher."

Dakota moved closer. Even without the wig, Dakota was

flirting, tilting her head down and looking up into Nina's eyes, hoping this made her look sexy. She was picturing Marilyn Monroe on the couch with Tony Curtis in *Some Like it Hot*.

She breathed, "So, teach me."

Nina looked at her with genuine concern.

She stopped.

"I know I look a lot older. I always have."

"The wig helped."

"I know."

"Are you safe, Sinclair? No one is hurting you?" She cupped Sinclair's face in her hands, trying to read through the flesh to her brain. Dakota wanted to kiss her. She also wanted to laugh. This is what they always asked in a doctor's office. Weight, height, blood pressure, is anyone hurting you?

"No, no." She didn't take her eyes off Nina's. "Not physically."

Nina removed her hands. What would she have to do to get them back?

"Well, why then? The wig, the name?"

"It's a long story."

She lowered her eyes. She sat still, like you do when you're afraid to startle a small animal. Nina was small. She wanted to pet her. And she wanted Nina to hold her again.

"Dangerous? Or just messy?"

"Messy." She wished she could put the wig back on.

"Jesus, Dakota. I mean Sinclair."

"I know it's a lot," she sighed. "In the bathroom, when I was crying, you never asked me any questions. You just held me. It's what I needed."

Sinclair moved closer to her again. "I need something different now."

Her boldness shocked her. She was full of surprises today. She saw her mother's face in the kitchen when she'd said, "You *are* my daughter."

She knew two things for sure: Nina was kind, and Nina wanted her. Everything else was chaos. The internal Sinclair didn't match the external Sinclair. Dakota was a better fit.

"We need to wait 'til your eighteen."

"Really?"

"Really, Sinclair."

"Look at me," she said. Look at...*ME*, she thought, but didn't say.

Nina's face was an emotional canvas that she was busily interpreting, and projecting onto. It was so quiet. She heard breathing, heartbeats, the rush of blood in her ears. She thought she might faint.

"Call me Dakota," she whispered. She leaned in and kissed Nina softly on the mouth.

* * *

"So, what would I like about her?" Howard repeated.

Sinclair smiled to herself. He didn't like that look one bit.

"She's funny—you like funny—and smart. She's pretty. Pretty and short, actually. I tower over her. Mostly, you'd like her because she's kind, and she's good to me."

"I like that last part. How did you meet her?"

"At a movie theater. We'd both just seen the same movie and started talking about it. Oh, and she likes *Badlands*. You gotta like her for that, right?"

Sinclair stopped.

"And her name is Nina?"

"Yes."

"You mentioned she has an apartment. How old is Nina?"

Sinclair sighed. "This is the part you won't like... But, it doesn't really matter, does it? Because the person she is, is all that counts. And I know you will like the person she is."

"What? She's sixty-five?"

Sinclair laughed.

"Too young?"

"*Daaad*!"

"So?"

"She's twenty-five."

Now the words rushed out excitedly, worried that he wouldn't be persuaded.

"But that's why it's perfect because she's mature—she anchors me. She was wonderful when I was a mess—she didn't even know me, and she knew how to calm me down. I can be myself with her."

He was desperately trying to think about what to say. He didn't want to ruin this conversation. But twenty-five! Sinclair was seven-fucking-teen! The age difference between them was not seven or eight years, it was more like decades. And he knew that a twenty-five-year old knew nothing either.

"You were fourteen years older than mom when you met her."

"Okay, Sinclair. Okay. It's just a bit of a surprise. I can't lie and say I'm happy about how old she is, or that you've thought about moving in with her—that maybe she's even offered. But you have a point about who she is, as a person, being very important. But you have the advantage, Rosie, because I don't know who she is. And it's really pretty new, right?"

"Yeah, but I already know I love her. And she loves me."

He wanted to groan. He wanted to not be a father. Not to be having this conversation. His insightful, daughter, was also, after all, a love-struck teenager. Probably first love.

"Well, you can't move in with her."

"I'll be eighteen in three months."

"And you'll still be finishing high school."

"Fine. I'll stay, but you have to stay also." She gave him a quick sideways glance.

And there it was, the tipping point, brought on by emotional blackmail and a desire to protect his daughter. Trapped into the decision he never wanted to make. But, really, he knew this would always have been the outcome. Solange knew it. T.J. knew it.

He sighed.

"Yes, Rosie. I'll stay."

* * *

I want to talk to Solange about Sinclair.

I can't let you do that Howard.

Why?

You know why. It would be totally unfair to Solange. You can talk to me, Howard.

You? That's rich. You're the one that's making this all happen!

You can talk to T.J.

Are you kidding? Talking to T.J. would be useless to me.

Glick?

I just talked to Glick. I don't want to see him right now. Just get on with the story.

Okay, Howard. I'll do what you want.

Right. When pigs fly.

I can make pigs fly.

Shut up.

HOWARD
THE DINNER

Of course, as soon as T.J. knew that he was staying, she was leaving.

"This is just a short trip, Howard. I'll be back in a week."

"Fine, I'll set up dinner with Sinclair and Nina. We can meet her as soon as you get back."

T.J. bought stuffed Cornish hens that only required she stick them in the oven. Sinclair was preparing the small white potatoes for roasting, coating them in olive oil and salt and pepper.

As Howard walked into the kitchen, he could feel the tension; saw the body language; Sinclair's slump and T.J's rigid back, neither of them facing each other.

T. J. put down the glass of Chardonnay she was sipping

from. He took the salad container out of the shopping bag and laid it on the counter. It had beets, goat cheese, and strawberries in it. Not what he would have chosen. Who knew if Nina liked beets or goat cheese? Why risk it? T.J. liked beets and goat cheese.

T.J. looked at him while leaning against the sink. "Where's the bread?"

"Shit. I forgot."

"Just two things, Howard."

"I'll go back out."

"There's no time."

"Of course there's time."

"You're incompetent."

"You're a bitch."

Sinclair, turned around, "Will you two *STOP*!"

T.J. took a gulp of wine and slid her eyes over to Sinclair. "I'm sorry."

"We're both sorry, Sinclair," Howard said.

"You'll apologize to her, but not me? Where's my apology?" T.J. glared at him.

That pissed him off so much that he just left the kitchen. From the open door, about to exit the house, he yelled out angrily, "*SORRY*, T.J.!" He was a child.

* * *

Why do you do this to me?

Do what?

Write me this way? "SORRY T.J.!" It's embarrassing. I feel like the Hunchback of Notre Dame, yelling "Sanctuary! Sanctu-

ary!"

That was a random association, Howard.

Maybe. It's how I look to myself.

Howard. I'm sorry...

You don't think, Miss Author, that you deserve a good relationship, do you?

Where the fuck did that just come from?

Well, you must not since you write me in relationships that are yearning and unfulfilled. Seems I hit a nerve, judging by your reaction.

I don't think we're in that much control, Howard. I think we blame the victim. Some of it is our choice, but a lot of who we're with is a crap shoot. Chance. Some people get luckier than others.

So you don't see patterns in human relationships? Cause and effect.

I didn't say that. I wouldn't be a writer if I didn't. But I think it's how those patterns get set in motion. That's what we don't have control over.

So can they be changed?

Well, Howard, hope springs eternal.

So you're saying no.

Actually, I am saying yes. Without hope, there's no reason to live.

Well, I guess you're just a cockeyed optimist aren't you?

I'm still here, Howard. I'm still here. Shall we see how the dinner is going to turn out?

I HOPE it will go well.

Well, in the words of The Rolling Stones:

"No, you can't always get what you want

But if you try sometime you find
You get what you need."

* * *

Sinclair opened the door and there was her Nina, all smiles and roses. And babka. She gave the roses to T.J. and the babka to Howard.

"Chocolate babka. How did you know?" he smiled, teasing.

Nina shrugged. "Beats me." He liked that.

"I love the roses," T.J. said, giving Nina a hug. "Nobody ever gives me flowers. Please, come in."

"It smells great in here."

"I hope you like stuffed Cornish hens," T.J. said, taking the roses and walking toward the kitchen.

"I'll find out. I've never had them."

"Tastes like chicken," Sinclair said, grinning at Nina.

Sinclair hadn't lied. Nina was short. They looked like Mutt and Jeff standing next to each other. She had a nice, open smile.

"Come and sit with us in the living room. Dinner will be ready in a few minutes. Would you like a glass of wine?" Howard asked.

He saw the hesitation, her trying to guess at what the right answer was.

"Go on," Sinclair said. "They won't judge you for it."

"That's right," T.J. said, bringing two bottles in from the kitchen. She walked to the sideboard. "Red or white?"

Nina smiled. "I'll have red, please."

"Howard?"

"Same."

"Me too," Sinclair said.

"Since when?"

"Since I was fifteen."

Howard just absorbed that information, like it was the most natural thing in the world that his daughter started drinking at fifteen. She probably smoked pot, too. Of course she did.

Sinclair took Nina's hand and led her to the couch. They sat down next to each other. Howard sat in the winged back chair adjacent to them. T.J. handed out the glasses of wine and sat down on the stuffed arm of Howard's chair.

The weirdness continued, thought Howard.

"I like your house." Nina said, looking around. "It's not what I expected."

"Oh?" T.J. said. "What were you expecting?"

"Judging by your work, I would have expected something unconventional. More modern and abstract. This feels very comfortable and warm."

T.J. smiled behind her wine glass raised to her lips. Howard thought she must be pleased that Nina knew her work.

"Did you know my work before you met Sinclair?"

"Actually, I did. I've seen one of your gallery shows."

Howard knew that Nina had just risen in T.J's esteem.

"Which one?"

"I don't remember the name, but the one with the naked figures that look ancient and dreamlike."

T.J. nodded. "I like you, Nina."

Sinclair looked visibly more relaxed. She beamed at Nina and without thinking affectionately slipped her arm through

Nina's and started playing with her fingers. Nina looked at Sinclair and smiled.

Howard could see how smitten his daughter was. It hadn't been quite the same thing with Solange because it wasn't first love or young love. It was less starry eyed, but just as tender. He felt jealous looking at them. He wanted what they had.

T.J. was also watching them. He had no idea what she was thinking.

Nina winked at Sinclair. It looked sexy when she did it. He was still upset about their age difference.

"Sinclair tells us that you're a high school English teacher," he said.

"Yes. I teach English lit to juniors and seniors."

It made him crazy that she taught high school students. His daughter was a senior. If they were in the same school, she could have been Sinclair's teacher. Why was their relationship more acceptable than a twenty-five-year-old male teacher being with his daughter?

"I think dinner is ready. The bathroom is down the hall on the right, Nina, if you want to wash your hands."

"Thanks."

Everyone got up at once, as if standing had been rehearsed. When Sinclair passed him on the way to the table she whispered, "Stop being so weird. The two of you are making me feel like we're a stage performance you're watching."

The platter of stuffed hens was passed, the roasted potatoes served. Everyone took salad, and the garlicky, hot, buttered French bread.

"Mmmm," Nina said. "I haven't eaten this well in awhile."

"Neither have we," T.J. said, laughing. "I'm afraid I'm not

much of a cook."

"Can't be true, 'cause this is delicious."

"Let's just say that the excellence of the meal is a family secret. And Sinclair and Howard helped. Do you like the salad?"

"Delicious. I love the combination."

T.J. glanced quickly over at Howard.

"A toast," Howard said, and cleared his throat.

Everyone lifted their wine glasses.

"To a most unconventional family, and our unconventional hearts."

"Hear! Hear!" Everyone raised their glasses and reached out to clink around the table.

Sinclair gave Howard a look of approval. Perhaps gratitude?

T.J. took Howard's hand and gave it a squeeze.

Thank God, he had done the right thing. The wine was beginning to relax him. He was thinking, this isn't so bad, right? Nina seems decent. She wasn't covered in tattoos and piercings. Her hair wasn't blue. In fact, she seemed pretty straight in her black jeans, white tank top, and buttoned jacket. No makeup or jewelry. Was this for the parents' benefit, he wondered? Maybe she's a Republican. Now, that would be unacceptable. The line had to be drawn somewhere.

"Who did you vote for in the last election?" Howard asked.

"Dad!"

"It's okay, Sinclair." She looked at Howard. "Al Gore."

"Hooray," T.J. said, lifting her wine glass toward Nina. "You are officially accepted into the family."

This was New York. She was gay. He wasn't really expecting a different answer. He actually was asking jokingly. But every category of approval that Nina fit into was Sinclair's hoped-for distraction from the real issue—the elephant in the room—Nina's age. He'd been offering the approvals for Sinclair's sake. Or maybe for his own sake. He didn't want Sinclair to hate him. Did that make him a good parent or a bad parent? He really didn't know. T.J. seemed to have no problem with it. As usual, Howard was the odd man out. Truly, he thought, as he looked at the three women, who were chatting in mutual admiration. He took anther sip of wine.

"Have I said how delicious everything is?" Nina appeared relaxed and happy.

"Yes, but it bears repeating," T.J. said, smiling.

She seemed to be enjoying herself. Everyone around the table was eager to please. There's nothing like food and drink to join humans together, make them feel a kinship, create community. He decided to join them. It was too much of a struggle to avoid being an asshole. For tonight, and maybe forever, he would accept Sinclair's reality, her choices. The fucking heart wants what the fucking heart wants.

"Solange," he said inaudibly under his breath.

"What?" T.J. said.

"Nothing." He shooed her question away with his hand. He must be getting drunk. He didn't realize he'd said it out loud.

"You know," Sinclair said, "Nina is a film freak like us."

She speared a potato with her dinner fork and another potato with her salad fork. She looked at him slyly. "Remember this, Dad?"

She picked up the two potatoes and started dancing them

in unison on the table, just like Chaplin in *The Gold Rush*, a film that he'd taken her to as a young girl. She loved the roll dance scene so much that it became a thing with them. Whenever they had rolls or ate small potatoes, he and Sinclair would do the Chaplin dance.

He melted watching her. He beamed his love at her.

Then Sinclair nudged Nina, who speared two potatoes and added her dance steps. Another pang of jealousy. Sinclair was sharing something so intimate between just them. He struggled to let go of the feeling. He watched Sinclair imitate Chaplin's deadpan expression at the effortlessness of those dancing kicks into the air, and now, Nina, following the same moves, like the Rockettes. He laughed at how silly and wonderful they looked. What the fuck. He forked his own potatoes and joined in.

"C'mon, T.J." He looked encouragingly at her and danced his potatoes over to her plate.

"Why not?"

She broke into a smile, looking quite young to Howard. Now the whole table looked ridiculous together. They laughed and kicked their potatoes into the air at the ends of their forks, but potatoes were not hard rolls, and they started to break apart and whole pieces flew off, which was even funnier. They were tipsy—maybe drunk—and making a mess, and it didn't matter. They were suddenly all the same age, and behaving like children.

"I wish we had a dog to clean up this mess," Sinclair said.

"I'm afraid you have dog duty," T.J. said cheerfully, getting up and clearing plates. Nina started to rise to help, but T.J. insisted they all stay seated.

"Chocolate babka, everyone?"

"Yes," Sinclair replied enthusiastically.

"Yes!" It was one of Howard's favorite desserts. Sinclair had prepped Nina well.

When T.J. stood behind Nina to reach for her plate, she touched Nina on the shoulder and gave it a small squeeze. Nina looked surprised.

She returned with the babka already sliced on a serving plate and another bottle of wine. Everyone else had had enough. This bottle was T.J.'s.

She sat down, poured herself another glass, took a sip and then gave Nina a dazzling smile. "Babka, Nina?" Howard had seen that smile before. What the fuck?

Nina smiled back. Was her smile strained? Was he reading into this? He looked at Sinclair. She was watching T.J. closely. She wasn't smiling.

After everyone had a slice of Babka on their dessert plates, T.J. lifted her glass, "A toast to my daughter, who has excellent taste in women."

She looked at Nina like the cat who wanted to eat the canary.

Howard instantly lost his appetite.

Sinclair stiffened. "Are you flirting with my girlfriend?!"

"What? No! What are you talking about?" T.J. went slack. How drunk was she? It was always hard to tell with T.J.

Sinclair stood up from the table. "C'mon Nina, I'll show you my room."

She glowered at T.J. and grabbed Nina's hand. Nina didn't know what to say.

"Enjoy your dog duty, Mom, because you really are a

bitch."

Howard felt like he was one huge jaw drop. He got up and yanked T.J. out of her chair and pulled her into the kitchen. She was compliant, like a penitent child. He closed the kitchen door. And then he screamed at her.

Sinclair and Nina didn't hear it because Sinclair had her music blasting, and Howard didn't hear his daughter ranting, crying, and then having sex, but he knew she was because, really, was there any better revenge? And comfort? And if he barged up there and caught them in the act then he'd have that image in his head for the rest of his life. And Sinclair would hate him just as much as T.J. Maybe more.

No. There'd been enough drama for one night. And maybe he was a coward.

* * *

No, not good enough.

What are you talking about, Howard?

I want you to write this scene from T.J.s point-of-view. I want to know what the hell she was thinking.

That's not a bad idea. Okay, Howard. Your wish is my command.

Right.

T.J.
THE DINNER

She was attracted to Nina as soon as Sinclair opened the door, and she saw her standing there, grinning, gap-toothed, like the model...Lauren Hutton. It was sexy. Something about her reminded her of Cherie. Even how short she was.

"These are beautiful, Nina."

Getting red roses from her daughter's girlfriend made her feel old. She needed a drink.

Sitting on the arm of Howard's chair in the living room she got depressed watching young love on display. Yes, yes, it was her own daughter, and she should be happy for her, but all she could really feel was the ache of deprivation.

She was looking at Nina's hands as Sinclair played with her fingers. The wink, and all that suppressed ardor because they weren't alone. It was a reminder of everything she'd given up. She drank some more, wanting to get to the numbness. She wasn't remembering the Cherie she'd broken up with, but the brand new Cherie, the just-met Cherie, when passions were high and the falling felt dangerous. Love always felt dangerous. She missed that. The delicious beginnings. All of them. Even with Howard.

What was Howard thinking? She glanced over at him. He was unusually quiet. Then again, she'd hardly said a word.

Everything was arousing her. Nina's thighs, her skin above the scoop of her tank top, the sunny, uncontaminated way her face was young and open. This was not a fucked-up young woman. T.J. had an instinct for that. She could smell the damage on someone. She was afraid that Sinclair would provide all that spice and drama. Probably one of Nina's attractions to her. Well, the daughter was a piker compared to her momma.

She emptied her glass, thinking, now she knew how her own mother felt losing her husband to her young, sexy daughter, his adoring fan. Really, sexual jealousy and competition within a family was one of those well-kept secrets, especially from the members involved. Frankly, she was amazed at how well Sinclair had turned out. Howard had done a good job. She had to give him credit for that.

The drinking continued. The three of them shared one bottle while she polished off the other. And then she went back for another with the babka. She was feeling pretty terrific now. The meal was a success; she was able to privately lust after Nina and no one would be the wiser. She thought she started losing control around the time of the potato dance. She let her guard down. She was too relaxed.

And then she touched Nina, and made that toast, and she

didn't know she had come out of hiding and was now visible. It was the drinking. Shit. What an idiot she was. When Sinclair called her a bitch, it broke her heart. She'd ruined everything.

In the kitchen, while Howard was screaming at her, her defenses threadbare, she just told the truth.

"Howard, I missed it."

"Missed what?! Missed what? Knowing how to be a good mother? Missed having any self-control?"

"I missed being young and in love, and having someone young and in love with me. It was hard to watch. It hurt."

She watched his face change. The purple rage disappearing. He looked fairly miserable, now.

"I'm equally guilty. I was reminded, too."

"But you didn't compound that by exposing your feelings, or by being attracted to your daughter's girlfriend. I am so much more guilty, Howard."

"Why couldn't you have just loved me, T.J.?"

"I do love you. But, not like that. Not for a long time."

"So we go on like this?"

"Probably."

"I gave up Solange for this."

"I gave up Cherie."

That was only a partial lie. She'd given up Cherie because it was played out. But she wouldn't admit that to Howard. She wanted him to believe she'd made the same sacrifice he'd made with Solange. The deeper truth was that she gave up Cherie because she felt threatened by the prospect of Howard leaving. She did it to make the panicky sensation go away. That was reason enough. She didn't feel the need to examine it. Just to make it stop.

They sat quietly until she broke the silence. "I think Sinclair will be okay. I think she made a good choice in Nina."

"How can you know that?"

She stood up and went over to where he was sitting and put her arms around him. She hardly ever noticed what he looked like, but in this moment she did. She glimpsed the old man he'd become in the hunched figure, noticed the lines around his mouth deepened by sadness. It upset her to see this. When had this happened?

"I just know it in my gut."

"She's so young."

"So was I."

He pulled away. "Is that supposed to make me feel better?"

"Look, Howard, the fact that she chose someone like Nina is meaningful."

"Nina is eight years older than her. I don't think that reflects that she's a good choice exactly. If Nina was healthy, why would she be involved with a seventeen-year-old?"

"Howard, she's eighteen. Three months, big deal."

"Oh yeah, excuse me, eighteen is a magic leap year into maturity. Why isn't Nina involved with someone her own age?"

"Maybe she is, emotionally."

"Are you saying that Sinclair is more mature, or that Nina is that immature?"

"I don't know. Maybe both. Did you think I was emotionally too young for you? Wasn't that part of the charm? Not to mention sex. Attraction doesn't come neatly tied up in bows."

"No, but we should be protecting our daughter."

"From Nina? From her own mistakes? If she were sixteen, or fifteen, or thirteen, I'd have a strong opinion. Or if Nina was thirty."

"What about yourself? Do you have a strong opinion about yourself?"

"Yes, Howard. Tonight, I hate myself."

"Make that two of us." He sighed. "But then we talk like this? And I don't hate you, I understand you, and what's worse, your response is also part of my own. So, I even identify."

"Hey, Howard."

"What?"

She took his chin in her hand and lifted his face. He looked at her begrudgingly.

"We're family, Howard. Remember?"

He removed her hand and sounded bleak when he said, "I wish the family of man could have just stayed in Eden. We were all just fine naked and unknowing."

She laughed. "There is no garden without a snake, Howard."

"Okay, then a worm in the apple. Nobody eats a wormy apple."

She laughed again. Howard had always been a man who could make her laugh.

FIVE YEARS LATER

Now what?

Time Marches On.

Cute. What year is it?

2006.

So that makes me how old?

You're 60. T.J. is 48, and Sinclair is 22.

Oh, my God. We're all getting so old.

It just flies by, doesn't it?

Are you going to keep using clichés, or are we done?

I'm done.

Can I tell you what's missing from this novel?

Sure.

There's no outside world, no news, it's like we're living in a bubble.

There are only just so many things I can focus on, Howard.

I'm not trying to write an unpublishable thousand-page book.

Well, at least write one scene that includes the news with some kind of reaction that shows these people exist in the world outside their relationships.

Okay, Howard. I just got an idea.

Why do I think you're laughing?

* * *

It was Friday night, and Nina and Sinclair were hanging out at the HH Bar. It was their 5th Anniversary and they always celebrated there in honor of the night they met. Who knew that Nina's book-lined apartment walls would become Sinclair's walls, too? How had she managed to go from freaked out, blonde wig-wearing Dakota to fairly stable, happily partnered, college graduate Sinclair, who was studying for her law degree? How did the spawn of T.J. and Howard manage to find and keep a normal relationship? She looked gratefully over at Nina, chatting with Allison, the bartender, who was pouring them free anniversary drinks. It was early yet and the place hadn't started to jump. It was nice like this, easing into the evening, surrounded by other regulars, people from the hood.

"I'm going to prepare a specific drink for each of you, just for the occasion. Age before beauty. Nina, you're first." Allison was wiping down two glasses and put them down on the bar.

"Hey, thirty-one isn't old." Sinclair put a protective arm around Nina. "I'd say, she's ripe, like a juicy, hot tomato."

"Good save." Nina laughed. "I was about to take offense at 'ripe.'"

"You say tomato, I say potato," Allison said. "Well, let's honor Her Hotness with a Bloody Mary and give it an extra kick of Worcestershire and Tabasco Sauce, perhaps a teaspoon of horseradish..."

Allison poured the vodka and tomato juice into the tall glass, added the heat, and then a dash of black pepper, celery salt, a squeeze of lime and lemon, dropped in a celery stick and stirred.

Nina took a sip. "Wow. Do you see smoke coming out of my ears?"

"I'll take that as a thank you," Allison said.

Looking at Nina, Sinclair pointed at her mouth, while circling her index finger. Before Nina could understand and lick away the tomato juice rimming her lips, Sinclair leaned in and did it for her.

"Hey, give it a break. I can only take so much romantic voyeurism."

Sinclair pulled away and sat up straight. "Yes, well, getting back to your original statement about 'age before beauty,' I would argue, in terms of psychological maturity, that I'm older than Nina, so in truth, my drink should have been made first."

"You already sound like a fucking lawyer."

"I do?" Sinclair smiled.

"I didn't mean it as a compliment," Allison said.

Still smiling, Sinclair flipped her the bird.

"Yep, I'd say you're mature."

Sinclair laughed.

"But, it's true." Nina looked tenderly at Sinclair. "She's always been older than me."

Both of them knew that was a lie. A joke between them,

really. In the early days, Nina practically had to re-parent her. She'd been a mess. But they'd hung in. It's amazing what strong chemistry can do, as powerful as the attraction of atoms, as mysterious as dark energy. You know it exists, but what is it?

"If either of you tell me 'she's an old soul,' one of the ingredients in your drinks will be vomit."

They all laughed.

"What the fuck does it even mean?" Sinclair asked.

"Only idiots say it," Nina replied.

"And now, Sinclair, if you will stop grinning like an idiot..."

"An idiot savant."

"...I will make your anniversary drink."

"I know what she should have," Nina said. "A Cosmopolitan."

They exchanged the look that couples do when sharing a private memory. And then they kissed.

"Happy couples are so annoying," Allison said. "Just makes the rest of us feel bad."

"Your time will come, Allison." Nina smiled at her affectionately. "Look at you? Sexy, long black hair, best tats in the bar, piercings in all the right places."

"You left out my 'up with people personality.'"

"Just about to say..."

"Something's happened!" Sinclair interrupted.

The news feed on the T.V. screen over the bar had caught her eye. There was a headshot of Donald Trump, in the upper left hand corner of the screen, superimposed over a scene with a cuffed man being taken into custody.

"Turn it up."

"Just breaking, a half hour ago the *Apprentice* T.V. show celebrity, Donald Trump, was shot and killed by a former contestant whom he'd fired earlier this season. What you are seeing is video taken by a fan on the sidewalk as Trump emerged from Trump Tower en route to his waiting limo."

Trump smiled in recognition as the man approached him as if to say hello and shake his hand, and then the gun blast was heard, and Trump recoiled and collapsed on the ground.

"Witnesses close by heard the assailant scream, *"YOU'RE FIRED!"* right after the gun went off."

The guy just stood there and in seconds, was thrown to the ground and cuffed by security.

"To make this shocking event even more macabre, the assailant was reportedly smiling."

Allison turned off the sound. "That's enough. I can only take the world's mayhem in small doses."

"Wow," Nina said. "Sometimes the bad guys do take the bullet."

"I've never seen the show. Have either of you?" Sinclair asked.

"No."

"Nope." Allison shook her head. "But wherever Trump is, it's always a shit show."

With the sound off, the feed was already onto the next nutso news event of the day. Sinclair thought, people die, other people make them die, some people maybe even want to die to escape the horror of what's happening to them. Becoming a public defender would mean plunging into the cesspool and trying to rescue people who get hurt, and people who are entitled to a legal defense even if they're guilty. The law was one of the few institutions that tried to hold the line and maintain civilization, no matter how corrupt its practices could sometimes be. She was idealistic enough to think she could do her bit to keep it clean and defend the underdog. She had a fire in her belly about social justice.

"I'll be right back." Allison walked down to the end of the bar and disappeared around the corner. In a few moments, Queen was blasting from the sound system and everyone in the place got up to dance, shouting the lyrics, "And another one bites! And another one bites the dust!" oblivious to what had just happened.

Allison was moving her hips to the music, yet skillfully managed to put the anniversary Cosmos down in front of Sinclair without spilling it. She poured herself a beer on tap and toasted them. "To my two favorite queens."

Nina and Sinclair raised their glasses, facing each other on their stools.

Nina sang, "And another *year* gone…"

Sinclair sang, "And another *year* gone…"

Then together, "And another year bites the dust!"

* * *

That was pretty random.

That's because you don't know who Trump is.

An actor? A T.V. star?

He was. Now, he's the President of the United States.

Are you kidding me?

I just saved the world.

That's pretty grandiose.

My imagination is powerful.

Have you taken your meds?

No, I haven't. Thanks for reminding me.

Why do you want him dead?

Because Trump is a really, really bad man.

Use your big words. Why are talking like this?

Because that's the way Trump talks.

You said he's the President?

Yes. Bigly. Hugely.

What's wrong with you?

Nothing that impeachment couldn't fix.

Don't say anything else incriminating. I would like you to finish this book before you're sent to the gulag.

So would I, Howard. So would I.

Wait a minute.

What now?

You said, Trump is President.

Yes.

So this didn't really happen.

That's why it's called fiction, Howard.

But, why did you write it?

Because it was beyond satisfying to have him killed off before he could savage the world. It was cathartic. It's the only power I have. In the real world I feel helpless. Writing this was a heady experience. As I wrote, I giggled.

Okay, now that you've had your fun, can we get back to my reality? What's happening now?

You tell me, Howard.

Well, apparently, Sinclair managed to survive us, and re-

markably, she's in a stable relationship with Nina, and...

Sorry to interrupt, but I already know all that. Tell me what's going on with you.

Well, since T.J.'s traveling a lot, quite predictably, she's having affairs again. I really don't give a shit. We get along much better. I'm pretty much alone.

What do you do?

A lot of nothing. I go into the city most days. I walk. I read. I do the occasional freelance film or theater review. I sit in coffee shops and watch people. When the weather is good, I sit outside. I go to movies and plays.

No music?

Rarely. It's kind of too painful. Seldom see friends.

That's too bad.

It's really not a terrible life.

* * *

Howard noticed that he was waking up more and more frequently to pee. And not just that, even though it felt urgent, it was hard to get started, like he was stopped up. It hurt.

"Go to the doctor, Howard."

"I hate doctors, you know that, T.J."

He was spreading almond butter on a piece of baguette.

"But sometimes, Howard, we have to go to the nice doctors because we have no fucking idea what's wrong with us."

She put her finger into the open jar of almond butter, and popped it in her mouth.

"It's probably a bladder infection," she said, licking her finger. "God knows I've had enough of them to recognize the symptoms." T.J. took another finger full and held it in front of his mouth. "Say ah!"

He opened his mouth and T.J. stuck her finger in. He closed his lips around her finger and sucked and licked the butter off before letting it go.

"Just the way you like it," she smiled, looking into his eyes.

They still had sex, not a lot, not often. Ever since he left Solange five years ago, this had been his reward. But he noticed with a great deal of alarm that he wasn't getting an erection. T.J. behaving this way was a sure-fire hard-on starter. What the fuck was wrong with him?!

T.J. pulled back in her seat, realizing he wasn't turned on. She got up and walked to the sink to rinse her hands. "Don't wait, Howard. It can go into your kidneys and then you'll really know what feeling sick is."

"Okay," he said, trying to control his fear.

He had early stage bladder cancer. He needed surgery. It was curable, but maybe only temporarily. It could come back. He would have to be monitored for the rest of his life. The surgery would remove the tumor that hadn't penetrated into the bladder wall. Chemo, radiation, but apart from suffering, it was not the worst cancer outcome. That could happen in the future, or he could die from some other body betrayal because, sooner or later, something killed you.

He told T.J. he didn't want her to visit him in the hospital. He told Sinclair the same thing. He minimized the experience. He lied about his attitude. He couldn't quite explain, even to himself, why he was appalled at the idea of them being there, of being seen when he was ill and reduced. It felt needy. It felt humiliating.

It would have been okay if Solange visited.

He let go of the thought, like letting go of the string of a balloon; a startled little boy crying because he didn't know this loss could happen. That it could happen to him.

Lying in bed at New York Presbyterian, Lower Manhattan Cancer Center, waiting to be prepped for surgery, having talked to the anesthesiologist and the surgeon, he was really frightened. Going unconscious and losing control was what was immediately scaring him. He was at the mercy of his body, like some thug threatening him. You do this, or we'll kill you, see? Won't get to see the wife and kid anymore, see?

He just wanted his body to go back to being a functional suitcase to carry him around—efficiently packed, well maintained, hard bodied, able to take the knocks.

These were his ploys to distract and entertain himself, but of course it wasn't working. His blood was too contaminated with his black worry: What if he died?

And if he died—an unanticipated drug reaction, a horrible surgical mistake—he would cease to exist. Never be Howard again. He had sometimes thought that nothingness would be a relief. He could lay his burden of self down: death as the biggest painkiller, the big Bayer aspirin in the sky.

But, most of the time there was no acceptance about it. Just rage. This can't be happening.

And then he woke up in his hospital room, feeling like shit. He was alone. He wasn't dead. The beat goes on. It was the way it should always be: a never-ending story.

Having achieved consciousness and regained self, he was now embedded in his suffering body. Oh, God, he moaned.

Pain was accompanied by despair. He was so perverse. Not glad to be alive, but bitter about being alone at his most vulnerable, and he had refused the comfort of the people he loved.

A drug was making him so nauseated that he balled himself into a small wounded animal, hiding out in his flesh, fearfully watching and waiting for this to all stop. As he swooned in and out of consciousness, he couldn't advocate for himself. He'd press the call button, maybe too many times? But when someone didn't instantly appear, he felt helpless.

He needed water, he needed his hand held, he needed to know T.J. was there, and that Sinclair cared enough to show up despite his wishes. Why did they listen to him? He practically demanded they stay away.

He'd done this to himself. He'd rationalized his needs out of existence. Not necessary, no big deal, he'd really prefer they didn't... He knew Sinclair was busy studying for exams, that T.J. was consumed by her new show. He was a burden, an inconvenience. No, he didn't need them.

But he did. In some dimmed, fluorescent-lit hour of the night he wept, awakened from a dream where he felt himself pushed from behind and he fell, falling for a long time until he landed into a pond of wet scum. He felt soiled, desecrated. He heard his mother's judgmental voice, "It's only dirt, Howard. It's only dirt."

What a fool he was. He thought he was being protective of his family. Being strong for them. But playing his family role meant that he didn't get what he needed. Couldn't ask. Pretended it didn't matter. The pain he felt from their compliance with his demand to stay away was more crushing than the physical pain. Perversely, he blamed them for this betrayal that was his own fault. His reasoning would go round and round in this circular argument, with him at the beginning and him at the end. He grieved for his losses. He thought of Solange. She would have come. She wouldn't have listened to him telling her to stay away. He despaired about having made the wrong choice. And what did it mean about who Sinclair was? Was it that she was twenty-two? Or was it that she actually didn't care? Fuck him. He could die now. He had served his purpose.

These were his darkest hallucinatory thoughts. But as he started to feel better, as he started to recover himself, his strength and hope, he changed his mind again. Protecting them from being frightened by seeing him this way was the right thing to have done. And during his recovery, his treatments, his improved health, he became more certain as he cloaked himself in this persona, as he picked up his protections and slipped back into his psychic skin, as he felt better, that he'd been right after all. He had protected them from looking into his abyss and by being frightened by their own.

* * *

Okay, I fucking hate you.

Goddamn, Howard, you know how to spoil a mood.

We've already had this conversation. It isn't me. It's you that spoils it.

It's just a part of life Howard. You get sick and you die.

I don't want to die.

Nobody wants to die.

People who commit suicide want to die.

Well, they wouldn't kill themselves if their lives didn't suck.

Define suck.

Yes, one person's depression is another person's motivation to change. We're all different. Our pain thresholds are different.

If you're going to have me die, I'd rather kill myself.

Why?

Done by my own volition. I'm not lying around waiting for you to finish me off.

That's pretty funny, Howard.

What's funny about it?

You know what.

Oh, right. I don't have any volition. I'm begging you to let me live.

Of course you'll live.

I will? What then?

What it's like in real life, the erosion, and progression over time. The deepening of attachments, some wisdom, and healing, moments of love, and the bewildering sameness that feels like fate, but isn't. It's just us, the same us, maybe a happier version or a gloomier version.

Or it can feel like doom.

Howard, every time a raindrop falls a flower grows.

That's pretty sappy.

It was a song lyric. A huge hit. The people's musical comfort food. It had a lot of melodic swell.

Tell me another.

Climb every mountain, Ford every stream, Follow every rainbow, 'til you find your dream. Bombast. Big voice, big fin-

ish.

> *You're kidding me.*
> *I kid you not.*
> *So, I'm not going to die.*
> *No, but somebody else will.*

* * *

T.J. got a call. Your mother is dying. That wasn't the conversation exactly, but it was the gist. As next of kin, it was her responsibility to make the arrangements. Didn't she want to be there?

When she arrived, her mother was in a coma. Her face was already like a death mask. She photographed her mother in black and white over the next forty-eight hours, as her mother's toes curled and her breathing became shallow. She argued with the nurse to give her mother more morphine whenever she saw a crease between her brows, imagining it was the only way her mother could express pain. As she sat and watched her she tried to imagine what dying was like. How much did her mother know? Was there pure panic inside, or just a shutting down that had no fear accompanying it, because the relief was greater? What did it feel like to let go? What is surrender like? Is it welcome? Does the brain bathe you in endorphins so that the final release is a happy one? Or is the design perverse to the end and you are conscious of your own paralysis and loss? She thought of her childhood dream, falling into that hole and feeling herself disappear, to cease being T.J., or human.

She was out of the room when her mother died. She had

taken a much-needed break after sitting vigil for so many hours. When she walked back in and saw her stilled mother, she couldn't account for her disappearance. It was impossible to understand how the corporal was transformed from mother to not mother, at the end of a breath.

She thought of a Victorian painting that she loved—a florid bouquet in a vase, a piece of fruit, cut open and rotting, a fly feeding.

She pulled her wallet from her bag and from a hidden sleeve she removed an old photo. It was a black and white shot of her mother and father in their glory days. Her mother's swan-like beauty, her soft white plumage, pressed against her father's black pants, his arm around her waist. Her mother looked mildly surprised. Surprised that this was her life? According to the date of the photo, she was already pregnant.

She always wondered, was it better between them after she'd left? They didn't divorce. Why?

She spent the next half hour taking photos of that face. And then she called the mortuary to have the body taken away, signed the death certificate, and made arrangements for the cremation.

She slept badly. She stood outside herself, amazed that she didn't feel anything. And then she woke up, and she still didn't feel anything. She just felt normal. Although, Howard said, she'd become hectic since she'd been home; her restlessness was annoying to live with. There was too much T.J. energy in the house, driving him out into the street on long walks to get away from her.

The way she saw it, she had a new sense of urgency—life was short and then you died. She knew that once she got back to work this energy would get channeled. Until then there'd be no peace. She thrashed around in bed at night; she walked the halls, rattling her chains and groaning.

"I'm calling in an exorcist," Howard said, chomping on a piece of toast in the kitchen.

"Truly, Howard, it's your farting. I think the gas effects me neurologically and I must rise and wander in same fugue state, drugged." She poured the water into the French press.

"I think that's the sexiest thing you've said to me lately."

"You're my Mr. Farty Pants."

"And you are The Ghost of Sleepless Hollow. C'mere."

She sauntered over to him in her pajama bottoms and work out bra. As she stood over him he put his arm around her and kissed her belly button. She leaned over and put her chin on top of his head, sighing.

"Don't worry, I'll settle. I just have to figure out what I'm doing next."

He ran his hand over her ass. She moved her chin down to his chin and kissed his mouth.

"While you're still deciding, you know, sex is a good way to blow off energy."

She sighed again. "I appreciate the offer, but you know what the coach says before a big game. We have to preserve our manly fluids and save ourselves for the field of play."

* * *

Alone in her studio, she opened the plastic bag inside the cardboard box that contained her mother's ashes. She lifted a fistful and flung it into the air. Her mother's dust, her bits of bones, fell into her hair and open mouth. She swallowed, sputtering and laughing. What a dope! She should have kept her mouth shut. Then she stood quietly, waiting for a reaction, for release.

She remembered the moment when she confessed—hoping for shock, anger, sympathy, protection—but her mother had just said, "What you think happened, didn't happen, T.J."

Then she'd looked away, stony-faced, refusing eye contact, but T.J. saw the tremor of her hands, which she immediately clasped to control them. That was it. Just a throttling, choking, silencing. Fuck you.

And her father, calling her asking about her life. Was she okay? Offering money, until she made a deal to shut him up.

When Sinclair was little, no matter how full she was she'd insist there was always room for dessert. They'd laugh, saying she possessed a second stomach. T.J. had her own second stomach used for the emotionally indigestible content of her parents' words, making her sick from the empty calories of their love. Her silence was caused by their silence, from their having nothing to say. She had nothing to feel guilty about. Long ago it gave her stomachaches until she'd learned to just eliminate their shit.

She picked out Nina Simone from her CD collection and popped it in her player, her spirit lifting as Simone's powerful voice crooned Dylan's, "I shall be released."

She'd felt different when her father had died.

When she'd hung up the call from her mother, she'd started shaking. Howard walked into the kitchen.

"What's wrong?"

"My father's dead."

He made her sit in a chair. He got her a blanket. "You're in shock."

She watched, while her body couldn't stop trembling. 'Too late,' repeated in her head. She'd always vaguely imagined that somehow, in some remote, fuzzy, future there'd be forgiveness. She had no idea how that would happen. Cutting off from her father was as huge as her loving him had been. When she fled home, she knew if she stayed she would become his lover.

He was supposed to be the safe parent. She didn't know who he was. He didn't love her. He loved only himself.

And then, in time, the world taught her that people compartmentalize. You can execute someone in the afternoon, and then go home and kiss the wife and play with the children and pet the dog. A good father. A loving husband. She came to understand that her father was not a monster—which was the not the same thing as forgiveness—and that the world was populated with monstrous human behavior. The wars and atrocities needed to feed the insatiable appetite for power and control. This was the part of being human that gobbled up other people, out of self-interest devoid of sympathetic imagination. "The Great I Am's"—their betrayal and exploitation of people in the name of the "greater good." Good for them. Good for nothing. Bad for everyone else.

And where were the mothers, for God's sake? Where had her mother been? Where was she now that she was dead? Was there a difference—dead, or alive?

And her father, who was now the Father, the Lover, and the Holy Ghost, was partitioned off inside her, stuck in an experience that had no ending. He would forever be succumbing to his creepy appetites. She couldn't reconcile the threat of his behavior, the shock of his kisses, with the ease with which she had reciprocated. If she squinted at it really hard, there was the equally squirmy, unforgivable thought: maybe a sliver, a shiver of herself, liked it. Which made her want to remove her skin.

She felt stunted by her experience, but she also felt knowing. Seeing the world wasn't a pleasure, it was a compulsion. Witnessing was where she came alive.

She began a new series. She called it "Surrender." She took the images of her dead mother and embedded her ashes into landscapes that, in each photo, surrounded her mother's head, or full body curled in her fetal position. She built up the bonded surface and hand painted it. The ashes became clouds, mountains, the soil beside a lake, rocks and rivers. In each one her mother floated. She was Earth mother, ghost, memory, the remains of the person who wasn't there. The critics said it was a mother's ashes mixed with the planet's ashes. An environmental statement.

People were shocked. She became famous. She was scorned and lauded. She was a celebrity. She had arrived. Her affairs became part of the public domain. She was a delicious scandal.

* * *

So that's why it's so important to her that I stay. It's because of her father.

Yes, you're the redeemer. Your love and constancy grounds her. You're the reason she can be who she is.

I enable her.

You're her private life. You're her heart.

And what do I get out of it?

You get T.J.

What's so great about that? A woman who can't express feelings.

Yes, she does.

Where?

In her photos, Howard. In her art.

But what about me?

We are still getting to you, Howard.

Still? Well, you've succeeded in depressing the hell out of me. Can we get back to something positive in life?

Like a celebration, an affirmation, and new beginnings?

Are you capable of that?

Yes, yes, of course.

I think you're the most cynical person I've ever met.

Not hardly. I'm a disillusioned romantic. Big difference.

How's that?

A romantic is a true believer. Inside that cosseted breast, beats a heart of hope.

Take me to the hope.

That would be Sinclair. She's a young woman who is about to get married.

THE WEDDING
JULY 2010

The extravagant house T.J. had rented in the Pines on Fire Island had a 180 degree view of the ocean from their bedroom on the second floor. Howard stood naked, eyes closed in front of the open windows, feeling the sensuality of the breeze and warm sun on his skin. He took in a deep breath, let it out slowly, and opened his eyes. The light bleached the oak floors and glowed off the knotty pine walls. A ray sparkled the water in the clear glass vase that held a fistful of buttercups. His bare feet made a shushing sound as he walked to the bed where his clothes were laid out.

He tucked the blue and yellow Hawaiian shirt into his white slacks. He would add the pale blue suit jacket right before the wedding. Later in the day, he could rid himself of the jacket, untuck his shirt, and go barefoot. He would probably drink too much. But he was more worried about T.J. drinking too much.

He didn't know what he was going to say for his toast. He wanted to say, "Rosie, you're the love of my life, and you've broken my heart by growing up and growing away from me." Yes, he was happy for her, but he didn't like the whole arrangement of raising children to have them leave you. Attachment was a cruel trick, nature's protection of the young, but nature didn't give a shit about the parent left behind, and how that felt.

There was a poster with a huge fish, mouth wide open about to eat a slightly smaller fish, which in turn was about to eat an even smaller fish, until, at the end of the line, a tiny fish was swimming as fast as it could to get away from the open mouth behind it. *Sinclair leaving home*. This was the caption that came to mind on his daughter's wedding day. His fears were the fish. The world was the fish. Or perhaps the fish was simply him and T.J.

She was still seventeen when she left him. A part of him would never forgive Nina for coming into Sinclair's life so soon; another part was beholden to her for rescuing his daughter. How had Nina converted water into wine? He'd expected damage and instead it was this miracle. He felt very divorced from this happening, having nothing to do with it. She'd finished growing up without him.

All the women leave. Was it better or worse that some losses were only partial? He was allowed pieces of these women, intimacies that disappeared, or even returned, altered, like with T.J.; a lifetime of not being known but being familiar, and predictable. And with his daughter, even she might come back to him as a parent herself with a new appreciation for him, understanding what it's like to be smitten with your own child, as well as frightened by your failures. It was comforting to think that most parents fail; a relief to know it wasn't unique to him. But some parents love better than others. Those that can't at all create the most ruin. He liked to think that he loved Rosie well. He just behaved imperfectly.

He sat down on the edge of the bed to put on the socks and shoes that T.J. had bought for him. Fine Italian leather, supple and golden, the socks, lightweight, 100% organic cotton and silk. He marveled at the sensuality of the shoes and socks, the caress of money. Not something he ever experienced in his lower-middle-class childhood, with the unremarkable objects of "make do" and second rate. He remembered his mother darning socks—does anyone still darn socks?—and asking him to stand still, sewing a button on his shirt while he impatiently wanted to bolt out the door. Everything was functional and repairable. His mother was the only sensual thing in his world. Her soft, fine-skinned beauty was daily chafed by the sandpaper life of a meat-and-potatoes husband and two needy boys.

Tying his shoes, he had an irrelevant thought—he'd always wished he'd had more children. Spread the love. Taken the pressure off, maybe. He wasn't sure it even worked that way. He'd never know. What would a son have been like? He'd never wanted a son. He preferred women. His world had always been a woman's world. First in his mother's body, then spending his childhood yearning for her, and his adolescence hating her. The years of insane, driven, hormonal need to get inside as many women as he could. Was there anything better? Yes, there was. T.J., and the bigger high of sex-soaked love.

He'd long realized his mother's actual death was merely a formality. He had already mourned her loss. Glick only corroborated what he'd figured out: that he'd married his mother. T.J. was another woman who kept him working hard to get noticed, to get his needs met. The only healthy woman he'd ever loved was Solange. And he chose T.J.

He was looking at his reflection in the oval mirror, adjusting the straw Panama hat he'd put on his head, when T.J. appeared beside him. She smiled as she reached up and lifted it off.

"Never cover up one of your finest assets."

He was surprised and pleased by the compliment.

He stepped aside and allowed her to stand alone in the reflection. While she studied her dress for the wedding, he studied her—the sea-foam green, silk sheath, her bare calves, her still firm arms, the luck of small breasts that defied gravity, the choppy, dark waves of short hair with sprays of white dramatically framing her face—a face that still, after all these years, captured his attention.

T.J. was not one to linger in front of a mirror, so having taken quick inventory, she turned away from her image.

T.J.

As she turned from the mirror, she marveled, *this is me—* the dress, the house, the daughter, the husband—but she would never be the sum of these parts. After years with women, she was having an affair with a young man in his late twenties, an ambitious young man who would climb her like a ladder. Her sexual appetite hadn't abated, and success brought opportunities that she might not have had otherwise. Howard knew. She'd told him. Since his cancer, their sex life had once again dwindled and then disappeared. The familiarity of his flesh, his wrinkles, his age spots on the back of his hands, how his fingernails were turning brittle, the slight stooping of his shoulders, through no fault of his own, neutered him. He was still a handsome man, but she had always found it difficult to sustain desire for Howard. In place of sexual appetite there was an animal affection that she felt for him, as opposed to the years when his wanting her was a burden, making him repugnant. But there was none of that now.

The Solange affair had been an exception. Getting him back lent the sex risk. There was also fierceness in him, all that anger-fueled passion that refreshed him as her lover. Over time, it returned to the same old, same old, and she grew bored. Still, the sex continued. It was part of the unspoken contract. But then her affairs began again.

"Why him? Why now?" he'd asked.

The simple answer was, Why not? As far as she was concerned, sexual attraction had nothing to do with gender. It was the light in someone's eyes, or their molecules wafting pleasingly into your brain, or perhaps it was the compatibility of stardust. Who knew? Why did it matter? She hated how something so elementary was twisted into something so complex. The incalculable, irrational chemistry of lust was perceived as so threatening to a stable society that it had been controlled, criminalized, and religiously judged for millennia. But nothing could stabilize society. It was always in flux. The attempt to repress people created suffering. When it came to sex, there were rules for men, but mostly it was the women who had to be contained. Howard didn't contain her. He had helped define her. She had been a vague, impressionistic sketch of a person and he colored her in and outlined her boldly in black. That's how it felt. That was the best she could do to explain it. Howard, on the other hand, was obsessed with questions of identity. Not just about himself. He always needed to understand, as if that would be the answer to life's problems. For him, "the unexamined life was not worth living." Who was happier? Him? Or her? And after all of How-

261

ard's worrying, and her neglect, Sinclair had turned out just fine.

She moved to the bureau, twisted off the gold cap from a bottle of perfume, and daubed her wrists and neck with her mother's favorite scent, Yves St. Laurent's *Y*. It's what remained of her mother's perfume and she used it sparingly. The mystery of inherited body chemistry made the scent her mother had worn just as lovely and fragrant on her. When someone hugged her, or came very near, it was a pleasure to hear them remark, "Mmmm, you smell so good!"

She smiled to herself. The convergence of career success with daughter gone and parents dead was remarkably freeing. So, it was something of a shock to realize how deeply Howard mattered to her, how attached she was. It had been a slow seduction, over a lifetime. She'd stopped resisting him. He wasn't an impediment. She didn't have to leave him. When Sinclair moved out, he could have left. He didn't.

She felt a rush of affection for him and turned to look at snowy-headed Howard with the hungry eyes, who had watched her every move, mourned her absences, hated her and loved her, who never forgave her, but accepted her. Why? That was sort of fascinating and surprising. It was as if the wallpaper in her bedroom had suddenly come to life. She'd never thought of photographing Howard before. Maybe she would now.

She had the impulse to touch his face and hold his body.

"Howard," she said, going up to him.

"Yes?"

"Sinclair is getting married." She cupped his cheek.

"Yes."

She put his hand on her stomach. "My body, your Rose."

"Ours," he said, unsmiling. He focused those intense blue eyes on hers and she felt his distress; she chose not to look away.

She brought his hand to her waist, then circled him with her arms. She breathed slowly and deeply as she held him, until his body relaxed and they breathed together in rhythm.

He murmured, "You smell good."

She smiled into his shoulder, pleased.

* * *

She finds me fascinating, "like wallpaper suddenly coming to life!" Wow, I can't believe you wrote that. That is so condescending. I thought you had more respect for me than that. Anyway, I'm not buying it. I think she's being patronizing. That last line of her smiling, feeling pleased—everything redounds to her. Even in this moment of intimacy she is appropriating, turning a sweet gesture into another moment of narcissism.

I'm sorry you can't see the kindness in it. It strikes me as odd that you're picking on this scene, which is relatively loving, to get upset.

I don't see it that way.

T.J.'s revelations are a big deal. Don't you like them?

Why would you think I'd like hearing about being neutered?

Well, okay, not that part.

No, they don't feel like they're about me. She doesn't see me. She sees this interpretation that fits who she is, what she needs to see—like she suddenly realizes her arm is attached to her. Isn't that marvelous. Move arm. Lift. Open. I feel diminished. Like she's won, and I'm the person left alone with any real feelings.

You've just taken T.J.'s insights and a desire for closeness and turned it into a win-lose power struggle. And aren't you just as guilty of the same thing you're accusing her of? Interpreting her.

But that's all any of us have isn't it, our interpretation of reality? No two are alike. Doesn't make it any less meaningful, less true. Not to me.

What do you want, Howard?

Real connection would be nice. The kind that transcends "He said," "She said."

I thought there was a moment of that in this scene.

For her. And I'm not sure that her fondness for me wasn't the same thing she'd feel for a beloved pet. 'Oh, Boots—there you are!'

You're so angry today.

Yes, I'm angry. She may feel like she's getting a big payoff, surviving herself and me. She can afford to feel generous, she hasn't changed a bit. She's now fucking a twenty-something-year-old boy. That hurts. She's only known capitulation from me. Sinclair is so lucky to have escaped.

You feel used.

Helping Howard. Helping Howard. How have you helped me?

That's so weird. I thought you'd be pleased. What is it you want?

I want to feel loved. Not just be loved. I want to feel it.

You can't just accept what you have?

Are you kidding? It's not even close! I'll tell you what I want. I want the tenderness of the dying; I want the kiss of the aurora borealis showering down. I want love to be the deepest cut. I want to be the center; I want the spoke of light to be coming from me and into me. I want to dissolve in a loss of being Howard and merge with the being of another. I want crescendo before the sweetness of the finish. And then I'll be satisfied.

Can I tell you something?

What?

That's not love.

I don't care. It's what I want to experience before I die. One last time. And you know what? You want it, too. That's why I want it, because of you. Am I right?

No.

I don't believe you. Doesn't matter, I don't get it, do I?

I'm sorry, Howard.

Can you now write, 'Howard and the Author sighed together over the disappointment of their lives.'

I just did.

Right. Thanks. Now leave me alone to brood.

T.J. AND SINCLAIR

T.J. walked down the hall to Sinclair and Nina's bedroom. Sinclair had never forgiven her for flirting with Nina. Their relationship had been strained ever since. Polite. Sinclair didn't broach the subject. T.J. didn't either. It was an uneasy armistice and one she regretted being the cause of. She was a clumsy cow when it came to being a parent. She could pump breast milk, but she couldn't feed. It was way too late for regrets about her life and who she was, but she was sorry about this.

She knocked on their door.

"Who is it?"

"It's me. Can I come in?"

A small, silent pause. "Sure."

She found T.J. and Nina sitting at a round oak table recessed inside a bay window framing the ocean; in the morning light their skin was the color of ripe peaches. They were drinking coffee and eating croissants, lounging in their sleep shirts and underpants, their bare legs and feet tucked up on their chairs, their loose-necked tops falling off their shoulders. It was a thing of beauty. T.J. sighed with pleasure, then covered with a neutral motherly smile, not wanting to be misconstrued. At least, she hoped it was a motherly smile. Come to think of it, she was not exactly sure what that would look like on her.

"Good morning, you two. A gorgeous day for a wedding.

As she walked across the room, she saw Sinclair hunch her shoulders, ever so slightly, while Nina gave her a welcoming smile. She walked up to Nina and bent over, giving her a chaste, familial peck on the cheek.

"Are you nervous, Nina?"

"Do I look nervous?" She smiled and stood up, giving T.J. a tentative hug.

"Come on Nina, I won't bite," T.J. said, and gave her a real hug.

It was a perfectly appropriate mother-in-law hug. When she held her at arms' length and looked at her, she appreciated the candor of Nina's expression, its kindness.

"Welcome to the family," she said, before releasing her.

She'd always been right about Nina. She wished she could be so lucky. Their breakfast tableau, and now seeing Nina's face—it was too bad Sinclair would pitch a fit if she proposed photographing them. She'd had an idea about documenting their first year together, all their intimacy and love, the ups and downs. She'd told Howard and he'd said, "Are you fucking crazy?"

"Thank you," Nina said. "I'm a pretty lucky woman."

"I'd say Sinclair was the lucky one." She looked over at Sinclair who was scrutinizing, watching.

"Thanks, Mom."

"Coffee?" Nina asked, sitting back down.

"No, no. I came here to borrow your bride-to-be for a moment. Sinclair, can we go out on the balcony?"

"Sure," she said, and shot Nina a look. Nina blew a supportive kiss.

One mistake, one night, she thought, exasperated. Would she be resented forever?

Sinclair unfolded herself from the chair and led her out the double-glass doors.

T. J. had a small package in her hand, wrapped in a brown paper bag with a string tied around it. It wasn't very big. On the balcony, as they stood and faced each other, she offered the package to Sinclair.

"I want to give you this."

"What is it?"

"Just open it."

Sinclair untied the string and removed the paper, handing it to T.J. She looked at the photo, wallet-sized, elegantly matted in white, in a glossy black picture frame.

Sinclair looked from the photo to her mother. "Who are these people?"

"Your grandparents."

"Really?" She looked back at the photo, staring at it. "They're beautiful. This is your mother...and your father?!"

"Yes."

It was the photo T.J. had been carrying with her all these

268

years—the black and white of them in their glory days, her life secretly taking hold in her mother's body.

"What do you see, Sinclair? I'm curious."

"They look like movie stars—rich. They're an elegant couple."

"What else?"

"I'm shocked to see that this is your father."

"Before I was born."

"Not at all how I had pictured him."

Sinclair looked perplexed, experiencing reality colliding with imagination. What kind of sleazebag had Sinclair conjured, T.J. wondered.

"But your mother is so beautiful!"

"Yes."

The unspoken, "Why?" made her ache. The answer, if there ever was one, died with the man.

Abandoning her self-protection, Sinclair looked at her with sympathy. Her daughter, after all, was, among other things, a compassionate person. Not like T.J. Not like her own mother.

"What do you see in his face?"

Sinclair looked again.

"I see a man who knows he's with the most beautiful woman in the room and that he would expect nothing less for himself."

"Where do you see that?"

"It's his smile—all confidence and shine. His body language—'she's mine.'"

"I'm very impressed, Sinclair. What about my mother?"

Sinclair looked again and quietly thought about it.

"She looks happy, but distracted."

"What do you mean?"

"On the surface she looks one way, but there's a small twist to her smile and the way her eyes are unfocused, like she's not entirely there."

"Bravo, Sinclair. You will make a great lawyer. Your powers of observation, your instincts, will lead you to the truth. My mother had just found out she was pregnant with me. I suspect that explains her expression."

Sinclair's smile was entirely open now. "Thank you for this. I can't explain why, but it means a lot to me."

Sinclair hugged her and for once, T.J. held her with a loving fierceness she never usually expressed.

* * *

T.J.'s winning. I hate her.

Howard, this isn't a competition.

Yes, it is.

You know, you're really starting to annoy me.

Wow, I'm upset because of my emotional needs not getting met and you're annoyed? No wonder you're single.

Yes, you're the kind of whiner that gets on my nerves.

A whiner. Then if I'm a whiner, you're a withholder, and manipulator.

Are we having a fight?

Does a bear shit in the woods?

Haven't heard that one in years.

Well, I'm old.

Oh come on, Howard. Get over it. Your daughter is getting married and you should just park yourself for once.

For once! That's all I've ever done.

We are having a fight. Unbelievable.

I deserve better.

You're mumbling, Howard. What did you say?

I deserve better—a better writer, a better story, a better life.

Yes, well this is the flip side of being a romantic—bitterness.

Is this how it ends for me? Stuck?

Well, let's just see what happens, shall we?

SINCLAIR

She was standing with a glass of champagne, sipping slowly, watching her mother move around the room of guests, all young gay women, all friends who knew who her mother was, but had never met her before. T.J., in her chic minimalism, all seniority and success, was smiling and flirting, effortlessly making herself the center of attention.

"Don't pay any attention to her," Nina said quietly, standing behind her, her arms around her.

"If I didn't pay any attention to her, I'd be the only one here who wasn't."

"Your father isn't. He's looking at you."

"Where?"

"He's near the door coming in from the beach. He's standing by himself."

Sinclair looked over at him and met his eyes. He had a

champagne glass to his lips and he lowered it and smiled at her. She felt a warm blush. He was still Howard. Still Daddy, but he'd been so remote the past few years. She felt like she'd done something wrong, yet he said he was happy for her. She couldn't remember the last time it was just the two of them and they were in that groove, where what they said was so funny, and how being together was as familiar as the smell of her baby blanket. God, the fights she and T.J. had over that blanket. T.J. would struggle with her to take it away so she could wash "that disgusting thing," while she cried and pled as though her life depended on it. And then Howard would intervene. "Just let her have it, T.J. Who cares if it's dirty or smelly. She likes it. It's not going to kill her."

"How do you know? God knows what germs and bacteria are living in it."

"Let it go, T.J."

Howard won, and in gratitude she'd drag her blankie and her sniffling self onto his lap and wrap the stinky thing around his neck and give him a hug. "I love you, Daddy."

Just remembering this made her tear up.

"You okay?" Nina said, looking at her.

"Yes, yes. Fine."

"Look at me." Nina was pulling Sinclair's chin toward her. "We are getting married today!" Nina gave her a radiant smile, touching her heart, making it race from the sadness of nostalgia toward a burst of relieved happiness.

HOWARD

Sinclair had turned her back to him just as he was starting to walk toward her. He paused and took a canapé from a passing tray to cover his embarrassment, feeling dismissed because of Nina. She had redirected Sinclair's attention away from him. He'd seen that. He couldn't help feeling the stupidity of his resentment. No matter how many rational arguments he made against his feelings, they remained beyond his control. He told no one. Certainly not T.J., since she would just not understand and, even worse, might tease him with it. It had never been a problem for her. When he'd railed about Sinclair's age, and Nina being predatory, she would laugh. Clearly, he was wrong. They were happily coupled. They were getting married. Really what he felt were the old rumblings of anger he felt against women. His life was spent being in their thrall in one way or another. He knew this occasion should be different; this was his daughter. What did he think? She would never leave him?

"Penny for your thoughts?" T.J. asked. He'd been so preoccupied he hadn't realized that she'd sidled up beside him.

"Not important." He took a swallow of champagne.

"C'mon. I'd know that painful puss anywhere."

"Leave it, T.J."

"Howard, it's a wedding. Try to enjoy yourself."

"Like you? You want me to flirt with all the young women here?"

That got her hackles up. "It wouldn't work for you, Howard," she said drily. "They're all gay."

"Your perfect crowd of fans."

"Not really, Howard. I do okay with men, too."

That was a smack. Why was he doing this? Trying to goad her into a fight? He knew why, so he dropped it. He wasn't going to make her the escape valve for his anger. He didn't want to make a scene. He quickly scanned the room to see if anyone had noticed their bickering. No one was looking at them.

"You know, Howard, I was feeling particularly good about you this morning. I was having very loving thoughts."

"And you're telling me this now to make me feel guilty for something I ruined that I didn't even know about?"

"You knew, Howard."

Yes, he thought, he knew.

T.J.

And now she felt deflated. She'd been having such a good time. Why did she have to pick on him that way? She didn't have to take the bait. It's like she couldn't help herself. He had always annoyed her. He thought she couldn't see him, but she knew he was mooning over the loss of his daughter; the wedding being the finale, when in fact, it wouldn't be any different. She knew that rituals and gestures were a part of his romanticism. She knew she should be sympathetic, but she just couldn't because it struck her as melodramatic and indulgent. Howard thought she'd never had a self-reflective thought in her life. She'd put it differently. She believed knowing didn't change anything. So why bother thinking about it? Only actions mattered. And despite all, she had chosen to stay and so had he. Why wasn't that the deeply romantic gesture he was looking for? Why didn't he understand that?

A tray passed with more champagne. *Hell, I'm paying for it; at least I can enjoy it,* she thought to herself. But now, as she looked over the room sipping her drink and observing all the vibrant young lovelies chattering away, her daughter and Nina surrounded by them, forming a tribe she was too old to join, she took it as an affront to who she was. When she truly was old, she would be formidable; she would never speak of it, never define herself by it. She wouldn't feign youth either. She would just be herself and own the body as it decayed, remaining in charge for as long as she could. She hoped what everyone hoped; that she would die in her sleep—at one hundred and three.

She liked that Howard didn't complain about his body. When he had cancer he was stoic and silent on the subject. He didn't want to be fussed over. She respected that. She also liked that in his eyes she would always be "the younger woman." Over a lifetime, Howard had been her looking glass. It's how she saw herself, outside herself. The image wasn't often pretty, or comfortable. But she didn't mind that anymore. He was her touchstone for truth. Especially now, being on the receiving end of a public admiration that she knew was shallow and fickle. So, when he admired her, she paid attention, she took it in. It actually mattered.

Where was he? She looked around, but didn't see him. She should find him and unruffle his feathers. The ceremony would be starting soon.

* * *

I'm worried about myself. I've been so...

So what?

So self-controlled all these years.

Long suffering.

Yes.

So, you agree with me?

Of course.

I don't know what to think of it. I don't want to believe my whole relationship with T.J. has been a mistake. That would mean much of my life has been.

It's just the way you feel today, Howard. Everyone lives with regrets. It's never the whole story. You'll see. You'll be in a different mood and life will be worthwhile again. Philip Larkin believed...

You really like Larkin don't you?

Yes, I do.

Okay, what did he believe?

According to his biographer, Brownjohn, he thought that life was not about "expectations glitteringly fulfilled. Life is something lived mundanely, with a gradually accumulating certainty that its golden prizes are sheer illusion."

Is that what you believe?

Yes.

Well, I believe that "All you need is love."

Yes, so do I.

That's a little schizoid.

"The test of a first-rate intelligence is the ability to hold two opposed ideas in mind at the same time and still retain the ability to function," to quote F. Scott Fitzgerald.

Except, those weren't contradictory ideas.

Okay, well...

Nothing you've said has cheered me up.

Things will get better.

Promises, promises.

Where's the trust?

Where's the love? Anyway, it's ironic that I was worried about T.J.'s drinking, since she seems very together. I'm the one that wants to get drunk. Very drunk. You may have to let me do that.

I'm still thinking about it.

Why?

There are two ways this could go and I'm not sure which one I prefer.

Well, while you think about it, I want to get back to the story because I don't want to think about it. So, where am I now?

Well, you just disappeared from the wedding reception. T.J. has left to look for you. You're at the beach, depressed, walking up to the ocean.

HOWARD

He'd taken off his socks and shoes and held them in his hands as he strode to the shoreline, stopping when the foamy water licked his toes and his feet sank into the wet sand. He stared at the rolling, blue-black sea concealing its inky fathoms where all life began, and perhaps where it would all end, in a dead ocean and a drowning world—its human spawn having evolved into stupid ingrates who were slowly committing matricide.

He'd once thought with joy about having grandchildren. Not anymore. He wanted to caution Sinclair and Nina. Don't. Please don't.

One summer he'd happened upon a decomposing whale that had been washed ashore, its fluke and fins tied up in fishing nets. It was physically and emotionally monstrous. It made him hate humanity. He couldn't shake the feeling. He slept badly for weeks. But then, it faded. He stopped thinking about the whale. This is how we survive, he thought. We forget.

As an eleven-year-old he'd been fascinated by whales. He read that fifty million years ago whales had been land mammals. There were vestiges of tiny hind-limbs inside their body wall. That blew his mind. He had pictured a mammoth blue whale walking around on two little hind feet, which of course wasn't the case at all, but was the first image that came to mind.

How was this possible? He researched and learned that the motive for these land creatures to move back into the planet's womb was food. Feeding in estuaries, they eventually adapted to go after the bounty that was more available off shore. They had evolved and left home, and then they continued to evolve and moved back in. He thought about himself—his vestigial hind legs that proved he once walked away. He smirked. Glick would have liked this discussion. He missed Glick, but they had really exhausted what therapy could offer him. He was left with his insights and his familiarity with his own character. After his cancer, he accepted his life, not with resignation—you don't get a reprieve from death and get to take your life for granted—but with an appreciation for it. Its smallness was enough, he told himself. Its smallness was a world. He would stay in the estuary. He would never become a giant whale and live in a vast ocean. Fine. The ocean was scary. It always had been.

"Howard?"

He smelled her before he saw her; the breeze had blown her toward him.

"I thought I'd find you here." She took his hand.

"Friends?"

He gave it a squeeze. "Friends," he said.

For a moment, the sun, the tangy air, the wash of sounds, the unseen spouting of whales and the silence of fathoms, the clamor of millions of years—the spit of time they clasped each other in—that was enough.

"It's time, Howard. The wedding is about to start."

* * *

You tricked me into acceptance. Despite what I told you. What do I do with my anger?

It's still there, Howard. You're still you.

And what about you? Do you accept your life?

More and more.

Yes or no?

Depends on the day.

I see. So because your life is unsatisfying, mine has to be?

Many years ago, my father told me, see this table? To you and me it looks like a table, but it's actually a collection of moving atoms. I've never seen the world the same way since.

Explains a lot. How old were you?

Maybe twelve, or thirteen. It was scary, really. It was like having a mental illness or tripping on acid because of the illusion of everything around me. But it was also exciting, even liberating, because it was the beginning of understanding the layers of complexity that make up life and the world and how very little we see, let alone understand.

Then what are we—me, and T.J., and Sinclair, and the others?

Well, since I am a unique collection of atoms, bacteria, water, sentience and cluelessness compelled to tell stories about the fragment of life, time, and the world that I get to experience, then you all are another layer of illusion that represents the world as I see it, in this particular story.

Why? What's the point?

Writing made me less alone, made me want to become more than I thought I was. Fiction offered me a larger version of the world and it helped me interpret the suffering and questioning I was obsessed with about being alive. It was a gorgeous gift.

I see where T.J. gets her religious passion about art.

Yes, I gave T.J. that part of myself.

Who else is she?

She's my father.

Wow. I didn't see that coming. And Sinclair?

She's my arrested development, my teenage self before Nina.

Did you have a Nina?

No. I never had a Nina.

And Solange?

She was a man I had an affair with, long ago.

Wow. And me. I almost hate to ask. Who am I?

You are my friend, myself, the men I married. No one in particular. My heart and eyes.

Your broken heart, your warped vision.

Perhaps.

You all have origins, but you transcended them, shaped by your own experiences, becoming yourselves, quite surprising me.

But you're doing the shaping.

283

Am I? What part of me is doing the shaping?

Yes, how does it work?

I have no fucking idea. To have so much power and control and have so little knowledge of what's happening.

Ah, and we're back to my life. As much as I enjoyed this Alice in Wonderland *conversation, you do have to finish this story.*

I know, I know. And I'm dragging my heels.

Perplexed?

A bit at a loss.

When in doubt, focus on the anger, the cleansing, pure, righteous anger that protects all the pain. I am in pain, miss Author, and you have to work me through this.

Yes, Howard. I'll try.

THE WEDDING

He was still feeling melancholy as he walked down the beach holding T.J.'s hand, walking toward the ceremony by the water. Sinclair and Nina walked, arm-in-arm toward the female Justice of the Peace, who had been ferried out for the ceremony. There was a bower of white flowers under which the three of them stood. Sinclair wore a white satin slip of a dress, thin straps showing off her shapely, muscled arms. In profile, her bare arm that faced the gathering was tattooed with a red rose and a green vine that ended above the elbow in a scroll that contained the name, NINA.

He'd been shocked when she told him she'd gotten a tattoo in time for the wedding. He hated tattoos. His Jewish cultural prejudices suddenly rose up in him despite the fact that he was a non-believer—he saw it as a desecration of his daughter's flesh. Jews believed their bodies were a gift on loan from

God and not personal property to do with as they wished. Of course he didn't buy into that, but the distaste, like an inherited food allergy, nonetheless remained. And of course there was the association of numbers tattooed on those in concentration camps. But also drunken macho sailors with "Anchors Aweigh" on bulging biceps.

She had been incredulous and offended. "*NOW*, you're suddenly Jewish?

There was no way to explain to her that he'd never not been Jewish.

Would he have been offended if the name had been Howard? Or, Daddy?

But seeing it, for the first time, he felt his anger spike. Of course Sinclair had no problem with it. "See," she whispered to him, "it's very tasteful and lovely."

He turned his attention to Nina, who wore a white linen, 1930s, double-breasted suit. She sported a white gardenia on her lapel. She was the pint of cream next to Sinclair's tall pitcher of milk. 'The Dairy Queens,' he dubbed them in that moment for his own amusement.

And then the ceremony began and they spoke their written vows, which cut in and out when the screams of gulls interfered with his hearing, which was not as good as it used to be. He really did need to get that checked.

And then they kissed.

"Are you crying? T.J.?" Howard asked. She turned her face and he saw the tears brimming from her eyes. He handed her the damp tissue he'd been using.

"We must both be having our periods," she said.

Caught by surprise, he laughed. Then he looked back at

Sinclair, at her flushed face after the kiss, her happy smile, the smile she had as a baby, which, for him, contained all the light in the world. He watched the tribe of women in their procession walk back to the house as he and T.J. trailed behind. Sinclair and Nina walked with their arms around each other, like lovers do, unwilling to separate. His daughter's happiness was palpable. He felt paper thin and worn out from all the tearing inside. He could be genuinely, unselfishly happy for her, but he couldn't vanquish the wounded part. What kind of father was he? Why couldn't he just feel, *Job well done, Howard; she is now someone else's responsibility.* He knew how sexist that sounded. He was a fossil. He was sixty-years-old; he was a dead man walking.

At the party in the grand, two-story living room where the chairs and sofas were taken up with young bodies filled with gaiety and laughter, where T.J. had joined the group, behaving charmingly, and for once deferentially, giving up the place of honor to Sinclair and Nina. He skulked around in the corners, the doorways, not mingling, too depressed to mingle, obsessing on his toast, and drinking. Howard had never been hardcore when it came to booze. He knew his limits, but tonight, on an empty stomach, he was guzzling champagne. Nobody missed him, or noticed him—the father of the bride, probably giving him a wide berth because of his foul vibe. Best to ignore the weird drunken man in the corner. Every once in awhile, Sinclair looked up and caught his eye, giving him a furtive look. He saw T.J. and Sinclair whispering. "What do we do about Howard?" he imagined them saying. Why wasn't his daughter bringing him in, making introductions, fussing over him, wanting a dance, wanting to say goodbye, wanting his blessing?

And then, sufficiently numb and pissed, in both senses of the word, from the back of the room, he clinked his glass with a spoon and started saying quite loudly, "Toast! A toast to my daughter, Sinclair."

And even while the interruption was still being understood and people began clinking their own glasses, he continued.

"But then I'm sure you had to know I would have to be Sinclair's father because Nina's father isn't here. As fundamentalist Christians, her parents disowned her. Their superstitious, cruel beliefs trumped nature's powerful blood ties, sacrificing their daughter to the fictional blood of the lamb. Well, thank you, Jesus for giving us another daughter." He raised his glass again and grinned in Nina's direction without actually looking at her. "Nina, I will be both father and mother to you, just like I was to Sinclair."

He put the back of his hand up to one corner of his mouth and spoke out the other side of his mouth, addressing the group in mock confidentiality. "And we don't even have to deal with in-laws! That IS a blessing."

The social anxiety of the herd shocked them into silence, giving him the stage finally. Now everybody noticed him. He approached them, swerving and sloshing his drink.

"Doesn't matter, Nina, I will be both father and mother to you, just like I was to Sinclair," he repeated.

"Howard," T.J. said, moving toward him. "Howard, stop."

He glared at her. She reached for his arm and he pulled away. "What do you want?" he said loudly. "You didn't want a child."

He looked back at Sinclair and now he was crying. "You're alive, you're here because I wanted you. I wanted a child, and you, my beautiful girl, are the love of my life!"

"What are you saying?! Why are you saying this?" Sinclair screamed. "I'm married! Nina is the love of my life!"

He bent over as if punched in the gut. T.J. grabbed him and started pushing and pulling him out of the room. "Howard, stop it!"

He clutched her. "I have given everything up for you," he cried. "I have nothing."

Everything was blurred. Was he saying this to T.J. or Sinclair? He looked up at Sinclair, at the look of horror on her face. He had put that look there, made her choose, as if it was a choice. He was her father, her selfish, pained father who made his own daughter bear the burden of his losses and unhappiness. And he called this love?

"Shhh, come with me, Howard." And T.J. finally was able to prop him against her and get him out the door.

* * *

Will my daughter ever speak to me again?

Yes.

How is that possible?

Because she loves you. Not that she understands. She may not understand for many years.

How long before she talks to me?

A long time.

Oh, God.

And Nina?

Nina forgave you even before Sinclair could. Believe it or not, she was the one to champion you with Sinclair. She was very hurt, but you're not her father, and getting over her own parents was a psychological achievement that made you a minor leaguer. She actually could sympathize with your pain. You wound up loving her.

And what about me and T.J.?

You scared her. She realized you were fragile; she thought maybe she'd lost you. For a time she was tender with you, as you recovered.

Recovered?

Yes, from your breakdown.

Is that what that was?

It was something building in you for a long time. Were you surprised?

More like appalled. It's been hard to forgive myself.

Everyone else has.

And then what?

Life goes back to normal.

You mean my normal.

Well, yes. But a bit different.

* * *

In bed together under the covers, Howard held T.J. She caressed his cheek.

"Howard?"

"Hmmm?"

She looked up at him. "You will die in my arms."

"Are you planning on killing me?"

"No." She laughed. "I'll be there. You know, 'til death us do part."

"You know there's no point in killing me, because there's nothing to inherit. You, on the other hand..."

"Stop being sarcastic, Howard. Just meet me halfway."

He looked at her. "You're actually serious."

"Yes. I wanted you to know. This is how I feel."

He could have made a joke, deflecting, because it was such a habit. Instead, he dropped it. He looked at her and said, "Thank you, T.J. It would be nice to not be alone."

"Not just not alone, Howard. Loved."

He felt stirred, because with T.J. he had never gone completely dead, but now it felt more like a habit than love.

"Why are you telling me this?"

"I don't know. Sinclair's married, about to have a baby, we're getting older, and I'm in a sentimental mood. She paused. I was thinking, Howard..."

"Yes?" He was looking at her in earnest.

"I think we're happier now."

"Happier?"

"Yes, you know."

He didn't know.

"More settled. Like this is us. It has been us and continues to be us. I'm not so annoyed with you anymore."

"I love that compliment."

"No, I mean, what I feel about you... I trust you. You're a good man, Howard."

Was he? He had to work on feeling that, like digging to the bottom of a collapsed tunnel.

"We're not always agitated by expectations anymore There's something to be said for longevity. It's our style of love."

She was right, and she was wrong. He felt gladdened by what she'd just said. He wanted to give something back in response, but then she'd never lived in doubt, she always had him. He didn't feel resentful about it anymore.

"I'm happy tonight, Howard."

"I'm glad, T.J."

"And you?"

"I'm content. A bit wistful, perhaps."

"Howard, you're never happy."

"Don't start, T.J."

T. J. sighed in his arms and let it go.

"Now, I'm happy," Howard said, and T.J. laughed.

He kissed the top of her head.

Lying there, he realized the tension in his clenched stomach was gone. As he focused on its absence, he realized his relief. When had that happened? Just now?

He heard Glick in his head saying, *Howard, this is what you wanted, what you yearned for. T.J. loves you. Not just the words. Your wife loves you. Your daughter loves you.*

...he didn't have to work hard anymore.

"T.J.," he whispered.

"Yes?" She lifted her head, and gave him one of her rare smiles that he'd always treasured—when she really looked at him, really saw him.

He was that hopeful boy again, looking into the sun of his mother's face, her disappointment now eclipsed by another face that emerged as the shadows passed; T.J. shining on him, beaming her approval.

* * *

Thank you.

You deserved it, Howard.

You kept your word. A kind of happy ending.

Yes.

Did you know it would work out this way?

No. It was just an intention I was writing towards. In fact, it didn't work out until the revision. Writing is full of surprises.

And Sinclair is having a baby?!

How does that make you feel?

It makes me feel hopeful, irrationally hopeful; in fact, happy.

See?

What happens to me?

Every time someone reads this book, you get out of bed and come alive.

I relive this over and over again?

Yes, but you don't remember. Each time it's new. Do you mind?

Could be worse. I could remember each time.

If I'm lucky, you will be alive after I'm dead.

That's morbid.

That's life.

But what about us?

"I'll be seeing you in all the old familiar places."

What?

Nothing. I have a surprise for you, Howard.

You do? Will I like it?

I hope so.

SPRING 2018

It was one of those mood-altering, glad to be alive, late spring afternoons, with a nip in the air, an azure sky, and daylight that was approaching the golden hour. He was sitting at the boat pond in Central Park, with his café au lait, reading a book of poems, waiting for his friend to show up. He was early. He wanted this time by himself to enjoy the lake view, the comfort of the coffee, the sense that he was in the last scene in a movie, where the protagonist is waiting for his old love to appear. He wanted to watch her approach, her smile of gladness at seeing him, the wave hello, to watch her as he once watched her so many years ago when she was young. When they were young. When he was young. Young. It sounded like an Asian word. Or a nonsense word. What will the memory of youth do to the present? Will she look the same emotionally to him? Or will the cruelty of aging shock them both into an awkward self-consciousness?

He looked down at the poetry book by David Schloss in his lap, and resumed reading from the poem, "In The Tradition of Men."

I had it in me to be that passionate
self-deluded person once with wildly
inappropriate women, but now I must
live without constant yearning and fear.

And even though I was happiest waiting
for everything to somehow turn out right
by sheer force of will, though we weren't
that well-matched, I guess, from the start,

it sped up my days and kept me up at night
when I poured so much energy into trying,
till the trying itself became an end in itself,
which tied me to loving like a dying animal.

"Howard?"

He looked up and there she was, standing next to the table.

"My God, Howard, you've gone all white!" She smiled and reached out her hand to stroke his hair. "It's very becoming. As handsome as ever."

He beamed at her, feeling elevated, reassured by her compliment. She would never make him feel old. The familiar way she was smiling at him made him relax. There was never any reason to be nervous. She knew him.

As she sat down and tucked her dress under her, the sheer material silhouetted her body, its pale blue flowers and yellow rosebuds floating down to her knees. Her gaze was full of interest and intelligence. She was just as he remembered her. It felt like the most natural thing in the world that they should be sitting here together, with time collapsed, as if they'd seen each other just last week.

"How do you do it? You haven't aged a bit."

Her smile broadened.

"No, I mean it. It's astonishing."

"My portrait in the closet, Howard, gets more decrepit every year."

He laughed. "And life in general? How are things?"

"Let's see. I'm still married. My children are grown, and I have a monarch butterfly garden."

"You're kidding? How do you know how to do that?"

"I read a book. I learned what to plant."

"You're amazing."

"Not really. And you, Howard?"

"Let's see. I've survived cancer, I'm still married and so is my gay daughter. I'm a grandfather." He grinned. He was enjoying himself.

"Survived cancer? Howard." Her concerned face was dear to him.

"Yes. I had bladder cancer. I'm alive, and here we are— God, how many years has it been?"

"Well, perhaps twenty years. But we've known each other more than fifty!"

"Impossible."

"We were impossibly young. Seems like we met in another

lifetime."

"I'm so glad you could come. I'm so happy to see you."

They stopped talking and just smiled at each other.

"So, you and T.J. are still together. That's an accomplishment, considering I'm on my third husband."

"Want to make it four?" he asked.

"Nope, this is my last. If it ends, never again."

"Okay, we can be lovers. I'd love to sleep with you."

"Howard, the idea of getting naked with anyone new...well, you would have to be blind."

"Reminds me of that great scene with Claude Rains and Bette Davis in *Mr. Skeffington* when blind Claude Rains tells a once beautiful, and now, physically ravaged Bette Davis, 'You've never been more beautiful.'"

"Yes, 'A woman is only beautiful when she is loved.'"

They smiled at each other again, letting the moment linger.

"I think," Howard said, "that feeling warm flesh under the covers, skin touching skin erases age. We respond, and that is the youth serum."

"Perhaps." She thought about what he said. "Yes, you're right. But let's not talk about sex. I want to be here with you, right now. It's a glorious day."

"Let's rent a boat."

"Really?"

"Yes, why not? Today is a French film. We should be out on the lake."

"Yes, let's."

He stood up and put the book into his satchel. He extended his hand to her and she took it. Her hand was so soft. So different from T.J.'s.

It was the middle of the week and there were just enough people to make it colorful, but not so many that they had to wait for a boat. She sat down in the middle and he stepped in and pushed off, then sat at the stern, picking up the oars. As he rowed, they passed other boats with couples and families with kids. He looked back at the shore. It was an impressionist painting. He looked at the woman he'd known for so many years, knew but never saw, the light shining on her hair, the light silvering the water. His heart lifted, happy to have this afternoon, a gift to himself. Her face was in profile and she slowly turned her gaze back toward him, probably feeling him staring. He carefully bent over and kissed her. It was a chaste kiss, a young love kiss, utterly romantic. In that moment he was in love.

He would dream of this kiss for the rest of his life.

* * *

Can I ask you one last question?
Yes, you may.
That was you, wasn't it? The woman in the boat.
Yes, Howard. That was me.

ACKNOWLEDGEMENTS

First I want to thank Atmosphere Press and Nick Courtright and Kyle McCord for giving me the best publishing experience any writer could hope for. Published writers themselves, Nick and Kyle, have created a refreshingly author-focused press. Kudos also goes to the visual team who made the inside and outside of this book look so good. Special thanks to Kyle for being such a sensitive editor.

To Michele Flynn Goodlett and Collier Goodlett--my extended family--whose generosity, food, laughter, and love have always sustained me. A big hug for Michele, who has been a beta-reader of mine for years and whose feedback I cherish.

To the wonderful writer, Kitty Zeldis, my lifelong reader, critique buddy, and dear friend whose commiseration and encouragement has been a staple of my writing life.

Thank you to Wendell Henry, Chris Henry, and Katherine Peterson who I've been lucky enough to have as another family in my life cheering me on.

Thank you to all my beta-readers whose comments have been so articulate, thoughtful and helpful: Nancy Dwyer, Leslie Powers, Judith Larsen, Michael Pressman, Michael Esterowitz, Dana Gotlieb, Burt Larrson, Jennie Fields, and Jim Cummins.

Thank you, Jim Young, for telling me to keep writing all those years ago.

A special thanks to Dr. Robert Pazulinec who was not just a beta-reader but was my psychological cheerleader, always predicting the published future of this book.

A shout out to a writer's dream residency, The Vermont Studio Center, where the time and space allowed me to work through one of the thorniest parts of the book.

Finally, my deepest gratitude goes to the poet, David Schloss, who is my best reader and editor. I trust his judgment about what is and isn't working on the page more than anyone else's. He's also family. The biological kind. He's my brother.

ABOUT ATMOSPHERE PRESS

Atmosphere Press is an independent, full-service publisher for excellent books in all genres and for all audiences. Learn more about what we do at atmospherepress.com.

We encourage you to check out some of Atmosphere's latest releases, which are available at Amazon.com and via order from your local bookstore:

Saints and Martyrs: A Novel, by Aaron Roe

When I Am Ashes, a novel by Amber Rose

Melancholy Vision: A Revolution Series Novel, by L.C. Hamilton

The Recoleta Stories, by Bryon Esmond Butler

Voodoo Hideaway, a novel by Vance Cariaga

Hart Street and Main, a novel by Tabitha Sprunger

The Weed Lady, a novel by Shea R. Embry

A Book of Life, a novel by David Ellis

It Was Called a Home, a novel by Brian Nisun

Grace, a novel by Nancy Allen

Shifted, a novel by KristaLyn A. Vetovich

ABOUT THE AUTHOR

Sally Schloss was born in Brooklyn, New York and has been a short story writer most of her life, published, unpublished, and award winning. She now lives in Nashville, TN where she previously wrote articles for music industry publications and *The Nashville Arts Magazine.*

Visit her at www.sallyschloss.com.